Individuation and its Contemporary Clinical Applications

This insightful book identifies key points of reference for the delivery of ethical treatment to patients with extreme and entrenched pathologies. Readers are offered an invitation to the intensity and complexity of individuation.

Written by a Jungian analyst with three decades of clinical experience, ranging from maximum-security correctional institutions to private practice, the therapeutic encounter is relayed in detail, describing case examples of patients who would not traditionally be considered natural candidates for the process of individuation. Suggestions and considerations are provided to enable therapists to support their own patients to find a point of entry into their individuation process. It also encourages readers to reflect on themselves professionally and personally, with the ultimate purpose of being more clinically informed.

Presented in an accessible way and featuring stories told that are touching and, in some instances, downright chilling, this is an essential resource for therapists and mental health practitioners, as well as anyone with an interest in this field of psychology.

Kerrie Kirkwood is a Jungian analyst and has been in private practice in Sydney since 1999. She also facilitates workshops and presents professional development seminars in Australia and New Zealand. Previously, Kerrie was employed with the Department of Corrective Services for 17 years, working with forensic patients and maximum-security inmates in the areas of addictions, personality disorders, dual diagnoses and grief and loss.

Individuation and its Contemporary Clinical Applications

Practical and Theoretical Perspectives

Kerrie Kirkwood

Routledge
Taylor & Francis Group

LONDON AND NEW YORK

Designed cover image: © Saskia Howard

First published 2026
by Routledge
4 Park Square, Milton Park, Abingdon, Oxon OX14 4RN

and by Routledge
605 Third Avenue, New York, NY 10158

Routledge is an imprint of the Taylor & Francis Group, an informa business

British Library Cataloguing-in-Publication Data
A catalogue record for this book is available from the British Library

ISBN: 9781032904504 (hbk)
ISBN: 9781032904498 (pbk)
ISBN: 9781003558125 (ebk)

DOI: 10.4324/9781003558125

Typeset in Times New Roman
by codeMantra

Contents

Foreword

The first four chapters of this book began as presentations that were delivered at professional development events run by the Australian and New Zealand Society of Jungian Analysts (ANZSJA) between 2018 and 2023. These presentations described my clinical work and the theories that informed it. The fifth chapter has not yet been formally presented. This book is a distillation of my clinical experience articulated through a framework that draws on both classical and developmental Jungian perspectives, as well as other clinical and non-clinical authors. While this book is not explicitly academic, theories are used throughout in the service of adding an understanding of the individual.

I have worked for 30 years with people in contexts that range from maximum-security correctional institutions to private practice. The experience of working with the challenges and constraints that occur in the therapeutic encounter has enabled me to develop an approach that places Jung's theory of individuation at the core of the treatment I provide. My work is with patients who have severe and compounded issues, as well as people who are struggling to live with the complexities that are inherent in the human condition.

Underpinning my work is an analytic frame that includes thoughtful focus on regularity of sessions, non-disclosure of the therapist's personal information, and a commitment and responsibility to the people I work with. The aim of this frame is to hold a space in which unconscious processes and primitive states can emerge and be contained safely (both for my patient through their transference, and for me through my countertransference). This frame makes it possible to reflect on these experiences as unconscious communications that may, in time, become the basis of a patient's capacity to symbolise. I refer to the people I see as patients not only because I provide treatment, but also to convey that my clinical foundation remains in the psychoanalytic tradition in which I was trained. Although I have an analytic approach, I refer to myself as a therapist to be inclusive to a wide range of clinicians.

I express my gratitude to ANZSJA for the opportunities to present my work, and to the other organisations that have been enthusiastic about the material I have presented.

Thank you to my ANZSJA colleagues for upholding inclusivity and preserving depth psychology.

My appreciation extends to all who have contributed directly and indirectly to what I have attempted to convey in these pages.

And thank you to my editor Teresa Goudie for her attention to detail and ability to hold and respect the vision behind this book.

And lastly my thanks to Katie Randall and Manon Berset at Routledge for their encouraging support and professionalism that has been instrumental in getting this book to publication.

This book has come to fruition through my discussions and supervision with Giles Clark and Sue Austin. Thank you, Giles, for your understanding of the vicissitudes of pathology and your lively ability to carry darkness lightly. My sincere gratitude to Sue, for your generosity and your endurance for meeting me in the areas of therapeutic discomfort and tenaciously persisting until these experiences were articulated. My heartfelt thanks to you both.

My family: I love you. To my dear friends: you are valued.

All clinical material has been disguised to the extent that it is unrecognisable.

Introduction

In my second year of full-time employment as a counsellor, one of the things a practitioner fears most happened: my patient killed himself. He wanted to tell his life story and explain his reasons for committing a contract killing that was described by the Judge in his legal documents as 'evil'. I was his only confidant, and we worked together in a maximum-security correctional institution for 15 months, meeting on a weekly basis. His final note was addressed to me and explained that there was nothing I could have done to prevent his suicide. He expressed gratitude to me for being "a very good listener", but this back-handed compliment still perplexes me and is a factor in the writing of this book.

My patient's suicide and working in the prison system led me to question the effectiveness of therapy and the validity of the therapist's role. During this time, I began to understand that a therapist may impact or influence a patient, but ultimately, they are powerless over the decisions the patient makes for themselves. Crucially, I learnt that the role of a therapist does not include giving personal advice or opinions. It is to bear witness to the patient and foster a separate clinical mind while being attuned to the relational dynamics within an ethical therapeutic frame. I have also learnt that my urge to intervene prematurely is almost invariably an attempt to gain a sense of control in the face of such extreme states as overwhelming helplessness and hopelessness. Furthermore, suffering is subjective, and what is manageable for one person may not be so for another.

Above all, I have come to recognise the influence of Jung's work and its relevance in the contemporary clinical world, particularly through his concept of individuation. In every context I have worked there have been several themes which emerged repeatedly. These are: narcissism, gender identity, sexual orientation, addictions, compulsions, obsessions and psychopathy. They each raised challenging questions as to how I could deliver effectual therapy to my patients who needed to come to terms with these issues, or the expression of them in either themselves or the people in their lives. My professional and personal enquiry focused on these themes and eventually rested on Jung's theory of individuation – and this became the central concept to use as a guiding principle in my work.

DOI: 10.4324/9781003558125-1

This book documents my experience as a therapist, and how I have clinically applied the theory of individuation. My therapeutic intent and responsibility is to support my patients to grow into *their own* personal and unique understanding of what individuation is for them.

My hope for the reader is that these pages will activate curiosity and generate ideas and questions that will encourage further self-reflective exploration.

Chapter 1

Individuation in clinical practice

Jungian perspectives

Introduction

Individuation is a central process in human development where the person achieves a distinct, stable identity, separate from their parents and the people around them. It is a self-realisation process, often discussed as if it were a universal phenomenon that happens to everyone as they age, without any particular effort on their behalf. The Jungian perspective presented in this chapter proposes that individuation does not happen by default – it entails the development of a complex, unique and profound relationship to self and inner-outer other. This relationship is dependent on an individual's ability to self-reflect, symbolise, and have an active and alive engagement with their unconscious. The fostering and maturing of this relationship between conscious and unconscious requires psychological work and courage. This chapter will discuss how to differentiate between someone who has authentically engaged with their individuation process and someone who appears to have engaged with this process. This appearance can mask a personality disorder under the guise of individuation.

The concept of individuation can be seen as relating to the fields of psychology, spirituality and philosophy. However, the focus of this chapter will be solely on individuation in relation to the clinical practice of Jungian analysis. The patient's therapy is impacted by the therapist's own process of individuation and for this reason, will be addressed.

The following quotes and summary explain the perspective of individuation that will be used.

Firstly, individuation is "… a *process,* not a state" (Samuels 1985, p. 102).

Secondly, every person's "… individuation story is unique and unrepeatable" (Stein 2019, p. 103).

Lastly, it is often the exhaustive repetition of thoughts, emotions and behaviours that invite or provoke an engagement in the individuation process. If someone defends against their individuation process, they run the risk of psychological stagnation, health-related symptoms and maladaptive manifestations in the form of addictions, compulsions or obsessions.

DOI: 10.4324/9781003558125-2

According to Claire Dunne individuation:

> … is the experience of a natural law, an inner self-regulating process by which man becomes a whole human being acknowledging and living the total range of himself. In the process the ego is ultimately faced with something larger than itself, a force that it yields to and serves. The human being thus recognizes itself as both material and spiritual, conscious and unconscious.
>
> (2012, pp. 83–84)

The attributes of a person who lives closely related to an individuated life are described by Murray Stein:

> The evidence of individuation is a broader, more inclusive, more integrated consciousness, one that is less prone to falling back on defensive operations like splitting and projecting. There is also increased access to instinctual energies, such as creativity. To keep individuation going requires a specific type of psychological attitude, … [d]epth psychotherapy is dedicated to opening up this space and establishing it firmly in a person's psychological functioning, so that it can continue being used for individuation after the termination of formal treatment.
>
> (2019, p. 130)

This reference is a valuable arbiter for how much integrity there is to a patient's individuation process and will be revisited later in this chapter.

The following seven points are fundamental clinical considerations and the quotes that are given at the start of each point are to provide a poetic and metaphorical dimension to the topic discussed.

The masking of authentic individuation

Andrew Samuels writes that, in individuation, "… the person becomes conscious in what respects he or she is both a unique human being and, at the same time, no more than a common man or woman" (Samuels et al. 1991, p. 76).

First vignette – Casey

Casey was a 29-year-old woman who worked as a website designer. She proudly explained having had very few friends at school because she was 'emotionally deep', which she believed was the reason why she did not fit in with her 'superficial peers'. In her late teens and early twenties, her only interest was attending live music concerts where she would fantasise that she was the one on stage being adored by the crowd and having the power to influence the way people felt. At 22, she met a man 16 years her senior and they were married within a year. Her parents gave their blessing to the wedding and appeared to revel in the wider public disapproval. The marriage lasted six months.

Casey declared she was bisexual when she noticed the strong attraction women felt towards her, which she then felt back. The assertion of her bisexuality mirrored the sexual orientation with her 'soul sister' Janis Joplin. She corroborated her psychic connection by wearing loose shirts that seductively revealed a tattoo of Joplin on her shoulder and informed me that she was born close to the 20-year anniversary of Joplin's death. Casey sought therapy because of the recent breakdown of her relationship with a woman. She was left bedbound and depressed as they were 'twin flames'. Casey's theatrical narration was just as intriguing as the details of her story. It was fascinating the way she would creatively inflate her internal realisations and assign them esoteric meaning. The significance of these meanings would be expressed with conviction and apparent depth, such as her wedding, her tattoo and her 'coming out'. However, after our sixth session, my intrigue had been replaced with indifference.

I remembered watching a documentary on Janis Joplin in which she made a comment to the effect that, "On stage I make love to twenty-five thousand people; and then I go home alone". This analogy of the stage stayed with me, and it dawned on me that I was Casey's audience. I formulated my reaction into a statement and, in response to Casey's upcoming date with a man that she met randomly on the bus, I said, "I feel like I am watching you on stage". She recounted that she had always wanted to be a performer. I then asked her, "What would it be like if there was another person on stage with you?" She refused to join me in this thought experiment and instead swiftly went back to the attraction she experienced with her new man. I noted her refusal and considered her capacity to symbolise.

Casey did not follow any social standard or 'norm'; she resided on the social and cultural periphery and always had since her early teens. The custom of Casey's family was to snub social standards and be anti-stereotypical which explains why they were so accepting and encouraging of her marriage, tattoo and bisexuality. They welcomed their daughter's choices and celebrated them without any parental reflection or grief regarding the possible consequences of unconventional decisions. Casey chased radical individuality; however, she was just living out the unconscious script her parents held for her.

Consequently, the decisions Casey made were ego-driven. She manufactured her choices with a conscious need to be remarkable like Janis Joplin. Her life's meaning was her solo theatrical performances, and her purpose was to source an audience that naturally extended to finding a therapist who would be a silent spectator. My disinterest potentially reflected what her previous partners and casual encounters had experienced. Once the honeymoon high wore off, and she had left the stage, she had no metaphorical internal home to go to – she could not relate to herself, or me, or anyone, without performing. The idea of being 'no more than a common man or woman' was what she feared most because experiencing life in this way means being part of something greater that is unknown and unknowable.

At an intrinsic level Casey was structured in a way that prevented individuation. Her focus was purely on the other's reaction to her: it was not on an honest experience of herself, or to be part of the wider community, or to experience something greater than herself. In the Jungian sense, the 'ego' is referred to as the 'centre of consciousness' (Hauke 2006), and Casey was certainly ego-driven. Her performances and stories were feeding her ego; she had no desire or curiosity to open a channel of communication between her conscious mind and her unconscious. The term 'unconscious' is also used in the Jungian sense and refers to the aspects of ourselves that we do not know, that manifest as repetitive patterns of thoughts, emotions and behaviours, and through projections, in particular of the shadow. Another expression of the unconscious is through dreams, imagery and synchronistic events (Stein 2019).

The heart of individuation is the acceptance of the reality that the ego is not the master and is not in control. Instead, individuation is a process whereby the centre of gravity moves away from the ego and resides in the ego's relationship with the unconscious self. The relationship between the ego and the unconscious must have flexibility and fluidity because the unconscious depends on the ego to bring its contents to consciousness. Individuation requires the understanding that the unconscious is greater than the conscious mind, and that the unconscious is dynamic and has a creativity to it as well as a destructiveness.

Life lived through the ego can be in the form of imitation, not individuation (Stein 2019). An example of this type of imitation is when people form a persona by identifying with another person, an organisation, a pursuit or a group. They neglect their own inner work and duplicate the ideas, methods, dogmas or theories of another person or group and make them their own. Another variant of life being lived solely through the ego is individualism (i.e., not individuation). Individuation encompasses the ego and the development of the ego, but it is not limited to this, it is much broader and inclusive of what is known and welcomes what is yet to be known. In contrast, individualism only focuses on the importance of the ego and its demands (Stein 2019). In extreme forms, this kind of individualism can present as a personality disorder.

The example of Casey had an obvious link to a personality disorder – there was an emptiness in her that is characteristic of narcissism. She attempted to avoid her feelings of powerlessness and rejection by making herself the object of fascination and desire. Casey had to imitate difference and defensively engage in performance to prevent exploring any deeper issues within herself or experience a not-knowing in herself. There was no opportunity for her unconscious to emerge as she repeatedly foreclosed any open-ended exploration. Casey demonstrated how inauthenticity can masquerade as individuation.

The magnetic pull towards authentic individuation

What can I bear to live with? A motorboat in the harbour or a sailing boat in the sea.

Individuation can appear to be subtle with the person showing minimal or no external change, while having an inner sense of profound change. The following composite example provides another presentation in reference to individuation and raises the question of midlife crisis.

Second vignette – Steven

When Steven presented for therapy it was like a breath of fresh air entered the room. He was light and airy while being grounded and warm and could comfortably share his thoughts and feelings. There were no obvious indicators as to why he sought treatment. However, at the end of the second session Steven revealed he was privately living under a 'black cloud' that would not go away; he reluctantly admitted he was depressed. This emotion was completely irrational to him because on paper he had what many people wanted: a satisfying, well-paid job and a good relationship with his partner and two adult children.

When Steven met his partner and her extended family, he was immediately embraced and having children with her was a natural extension of this inclusivity. Being an active parent and providing financially for the family gave him a sense of purpose and he relished in these roles for nearly two decades. Yet, for the past 18 months, no matter how hard he tried to push it away, the depression kept making an unwelcome appearance.

An opportunity for a promotion arose at Steven's work and his senior manager encouraged him to apply. Because he always did what was professionally expected, he submitted his application with the hope that a new role would lift his depression. A few weeks later when he was travelling on the train to the interview, he disembarked at the station and realised he had left all his essential documentation on the seat. He panicked and got the next express train to the city – he thought he could meet the train he was previously on at Central as it did the Central loop and hopefully, he would retrieve his documents.

This experience became a metaphor for Steven which he interpreted as wanting to leave his life behind and head to his 'centre', where he fulfilled his secret desire to sail away by himself. During sessions, Steven communicated clearly and truthfully, but the thought of expressing himself from his centre to his partner was debilitating. The reason he could not entertain her reaction of his desire to leave his job and set sail indefinitely is because he would have to be honest. He would have to disclose his apathy about her joining him and whether he wanted to continue the marriage. Steven felt paralysed; he simply could not find a smooth pathway to undertake his nautical adventure without disrupting or disappointing his partner, family or work.

Surrendering of the ego

The pain of trying to gain control will eventually outweigh the peril of losing control.

The engagement in the individuation process is rarely experienced as a choice, but as a forceful pull that one has tried relentlessly and repeatedly to defend against.

There can be the sensation of standing on the edge of a chasm and that one must jump and take responsibility for the consequences that follow. To do this, a person needs to be present to the experience; if this is not possible and they are to grow, they need to be able to process in hindsight their response to this psychological turning point. The person needs to come to a decision as to whether they jump or stand on the edge; whether they engage in the process of individuation or continue living in a way that is familiar to them. Often a decision is made when a person has tirelessly wrestled with the question of which 'un-lived life' they are prepared to live with.

Steven was on the edge of the chasm, feeling the pull to jump, knowing he needed to follow his desire to leave his job and set sail. This was very much in contrast to Casey who was frantically looking for a mountain to climb so she could be the only one at the summit and yell 'look at me!' Steven wanted his experience to be private due to the shame of going against his steadfast commitment that he would always keep the family unit together, unlike his father who had been married three times and left a trail of destruction in his wake. He was dreading the potential publicity this would draw to himself, his family and his colleagues, whereas Casey's decisions were driven by her longing for a public reaction.

Another difference between Steven and Casey is that Steven knew that what he was doing was irrational to his ego and he felt scared, and when faced with the choice of whether to stay or go, he felt incapacitated. The person who is genuinely individuating is aware of the jeopardy they are putting themselves and other people in and has a sense of relational and moral responsibility. They have persistently tried (often over a long period) to not do whatever they are about to do and have exhausted all other options. The individuating person often must fight against the rationality of their ego, which is very different from the person who is inflating their ego by seeking glory and satisfaction, be it fame, money, admiration or status.

This process is described in Stein's interpretation of Jung:

> In order for individuality to appear fully, an "assimilation of unconscious contents" (1966, CW11, para. 505) must therefore necessarily take place. In order to do this, the ego has to relinquish control over the contents of consciousness in favor of a process that is not completely under its management: "The assimilation of unconscious contents leads ... to a condition in which conscious intention is excluded and is supplanted by a process of development that seems to us irrational. This process alone signifies individuation, and its product is individuality ... particular and universal at once" (ibid). This act of giving over control to an irrational process, then, is the next major step on the path to individuation.
>
> (2019, p. 47)

This quote reiterates that the ego cannot have entire responsibility and ultimately must concede. A person's energy and direction need to be generated from the conversation between the ego and unconscious. Lucy Huskinson (2002) describes how the ego experiences this process of relinquishing control to the unconscious contents as a form of violence. The word 'violence' is used because the unconscious appears as an assault on the self-containment of the ego; this breach must occur for creativity to be possible. The unconscious is experienced as 'Other' by the ego because it is unknown. Jung describes the ferocity of this encounter as an unforgettable wounding:

> Whoever has suffered once from an intrusion of the unconscious has at least a scar if not an open wound. His wholeness, as he understood it, the wholeness of his ego personality, has been badly damaged, for it became obvious he was not alone; something which he did not control was in the same house with him, and that is of course wounding to the pride of the ego personality, a fatal blow to his own monarchy.
>
> (Jung, cited in Huskinson 2002, p. 445)

The purpose of this extreme encounter is for the individual to consciously integrate their inferior function that had previously been suppressed. The inferior function is an area of difficulty for the person that is for the most part unconscious, but when the contents of the inferior function are integrated into ego-consciousness, there is enormous potential for change (Samuels et al. 1991, p. 154). The ego needs to be reformulated through this experience of the unconscious. Also, one needs to develop an awareness of being both conscious and unconscious and maintain this disposition of openness thereby fostering the relationship between the two. Lastly, one needs to develop an understanding that destruction and creation are inseparable – a person cannot have one without the other and they are both necessary for psychological growth. Jung writes:

> ... the invisible things cannot come into being without torture and destruction for the collective man ... you always kill and destroy in order to bring something new into existence. Whatever you do, if it is of any importance, also means destruction.
>
> (Jung, cited in Huskinson 2002, p. 447)

Furthermore, Jung describes what occurs at the completion of this encounter:

> [It is] only through extreme pain (that) you experience yourself; you believe then that you are a unit. Before that, you can imagine that you are anybody ... you are not necessarily yourself. Afterwards when you have undergone this extraordinary experience of the self, there are no illusions any longer. You know exactly who you are.
>
> (Jung, cited in Huskinson 2002, p. 446)

For an individual to have the experience described by Jung of knowing exactly who they are, at both particular and universal levels, they must have the capacity to symbolise.

The capacity to symbolise

> Courage and the unknown are a revolutionary couple that co-create unimaginable change.

When the ego is overwhelmed by unconscious contents a symbol may be produced by the psyche that can bring guidance and comfort if the individual chooses to engage with it:

> When the ego is at a loss to understand, the psyche spontaneously produces a symbol. This symbolic framework enables the ego to relate to the unconscious experiences within it and protects it from the onslaught of insanity that would otherwise overcome it: 'You see, by means of a symbol, such dangers can be accepted: one can submit to them, digest them. Otherwise ... it is a very danger-ous situation: one is exposed without protection to the onslaught of the uncon-scious' (Jung 1934–9, p. 1249). When this symbol makes its appearance, the balance between the ego and the unconscious is restored.
>
> (Huskinson 2002, p. 448)

Steven's transformative symbolic experience occurred not long after his interview when he was on another train commuting to work. The train routinely stopped at Central Station, and he looked at the page of the newspaper that the passenger next to him had turned to, which was a picture of a sailing boat in the middle of the ocean. The black and white print all around the picture became blurry as he was overcome with emotion and became cognitively fragmented.

Steven's intellectual and somatic reaction indicated that the image of the boat was a 'symbol' not a 'sign'. For Jung, a sign has only a 'known' quality to it – a stop sign is simply a stop sign nothing else – whereas a symbol has both a known and an unknown quality. This is explained by Rosemary Gordon:

> ... this is what Jung meant by the symbol as a representation of an 'unknown fact' – not that the symbol was unknowable but that it expresses facts, relation-ships and sensuous and emotional experiences that are too complex to be con-veyed by mere intellectual formulations.
>
> (Gordon, cited in Colman 2010, p. 292; ital. added)

Symbols cannot be completely or successfully integrated into language or images. What is also important to understand about symbols is that they are subjectively determined. Looking at the image of the boat was profoundly symbolic for Ste-ven; it brought together the visual, the timing, the location, his psychological state at that moment and developmental life stage. All these factors accumulated and resulted in an unforgettable heightened affective experience that felt numinous. This event could be described as 'synchronicity' as Steven felt like his inner and outer worlds had collided. This image was subjectively meaningful for Steven and conveyed a sense of supportive reassurance but, for the passenger sitting next to him, the boat was a boat that related to a story: it was a sign.

Symbols often appear in times of severe stress or when the pain of life becomes unbearable, because the threshold of consciousness is reduced, and the unconscious contents are more likely to make themselves known (Stein 2019). A symbolic function is not something you have or do not have; it is a spectrum of positions ranging from the negation of reality, to the ability to entertain that reality may hold absence and lack. It can be described as the ego being able to hold what is consciously known, while being open and curious about the emerging unknown, the unconscious. Another explanation of symbolisation is when someone can understand that the fantasy in their conscious mind is absent, and they are able to grieve this reality (Colman 2006).

The ability to symbolise also includes being able to articulate emotions and use language to describe sensations, images, metaphors and stories. When this involves another person, there is the capacity for an interplay of communicative digestion and processing and being able to understand one's own mind while being open and curious to another.

Steven had the capacity to symbolise as he was able to distinguish fantasy from reality. His fantasy was to leave his job and set sail. Meanwhile, the reality was that his life felt empty, that he was 'going through the motions' and was unable to share his dilemma with his partner or anybody else other than me. He could acknowledge and articulate that not taking the promotion and leaving his job could potentially have a disastrous impact on his marriage, his social status, and how he was perceived by his parents-in-law and colleagues. The reality of these consequences was unknown. Steven was paralysed by his dichotomy that could be seen as the impetus for the communicative interaction between his conscious and unconscious that manifested as a multi-dimensional symbolic image of a boat.

In contrast to Steven, Casey was unable to imagine that her life (reality) was not how she wanted it to be (her fantasy). She adamantly believed that she was special and expected to be adored because of it; she could not entertain the fact that her fantasy was not a reality. In sessions she would negate the reality that I would attempt to offer and could not fathom a perspective that was different from her own. Everything had to be known by her and on her terms. Casey's meaning-making was in the service of inflating her ego whereas with Steven it was in the service of self-realisation.

Casey's tattoo of Janis Joplin was an act of imitation; it was a sign that they were soul sisters. She was unable to engage in symbolic thought and refused to imagine if there was any difference between herself and Joplin. Casey needed to fuse with a role model and instead of being able to explore her fantasies about what their differences and similarities were, she imitated and mimicked them to indulge her ego. The ceaseless self-referential quality Casey demonstrated was indicative of a disordered self, as she borrowed someone else's stardom and pretended it was hers. Casey was posturing as an individuated person, but it was a defence against her narcissism, a garment for hiding how narcissistic she was.

I return to the definition used in the introduction from Stein, where he states: "[t]he evidence of individuation is a broader, more inclusive, more integrated consciousness, one that is less prone to falling back on defensive operations like splitting and projecting" (2019, p. 130). In the therapeutic relationship, the patient's defence mechanisms can be observed and will indicate their capacity to symbolise. The patient does need a certain degree of ego strength to acknowledge and explore their defence mechanisms. Additionally, a strong-enough ego is required to consciously understand that their reality has an unknown quality and contains losses and lacks that need to be grieved. It is the process of grieving in the therapeutic relationship that can facilitate the patient building a sufficiently robust ego. This enables them to be in a position for the ego to surrender to the unconscious and potentially engage in the individuation process.

If a patient's ego cannot support adequate symbolisation, potential opportunities for individuation are missed and life circumstances that are presented become a forum to reinforce defences and entrench symptomatic manifestations. When a patient has a strong-enough ego, they can look back at certain times in their life and situations and acknowledge the missed opportunities for individuation. There is often a grief that comes with this historic reflection as it shows what life potentially could have been. An important factor to consider is when a patient does not have a sufficiently intact ego, they can be at risk of psychosis, as the conscious mind can become overwhelmed by unconscious material.

Living in a relationship with the unconscious

It is not I who create myself, rather I happen to myself.

(Jung 1970, para. 391)

The illusion that someone can *create* themself is a fantasy of the ego – it is a contrivance manufactured by the ego to elicit a response from the outside world. The *happening* of oneself is an ever-evolving experience of being in the world.

According to Dunne, Jung believed that, metaphorically speaking, "… people live on only one or two floors of a large apartment building …" and they do not explore the rest of the floors (2012, p. 105). These unexplored floors are fully functioning regardless of whether a person is aware of them or not. For individuation to occur there must be a robust ego (the known two floors) that is curious about the emerging unconscious (the unknown floors). The person must understand that their unconscious self is greater than their conscious self, and that their unconscious is dynamic and has a creativity to it as well as a destructiveness. Jung states that:

[t]he unconscious itself is neither tricky nor evil – it is Nature, both beautiful and terrible … The best way of dealing with the unconscious is the creative way … the unconscious, long identified as the oceanic in man, is Nature. The seeker of himself often feels cast adrift, setting a course between light and dark but ultimately moved by unseen currents deep within.

(1973, pp. 108–109)

Dunne goes on to explain that:

> [t]he world of the unconscious is essentially an ambivalent one, with both negative and positive aspects at all its levels, which doesn't make it easy to understand. Often it begins to make itself felt out of a negative state, such as boredom or stagnation in life, or a blow to the ego, a wounding of the personality.
>
> (2012, pp. 105–106)

A person usually seeks therapy when this kind of negative state becomes unbearable or when the consequences of attempting to avoid this state become undeniable. In the therapeutic encounter, the unconscious presents in the intrapersonal and interpersonal dynamics and can appear in the form of complexes, projections and projective identifications, some or all of which can be seen as belonging to the shadow. Dreams, images, synchronicities and symbolism are also communications of the unconscious that are seeking conscious integration.

During the therapeutic process the patient may feel exasperated, as they believe they are spiralling around the same issues and covering the same ground. However, this psychological circumambulation is not futile if there is a growing relationship between their ego and unconscious, because a more muscular psyche is being formed and the spiralling is serving to attain higher levels of consciousness and is gaining access to deeper layers within oneself. The consistent processing of this material facilitates a confidence in understanding one's own symbolic language. Also, a trust is developed in the emerging unknown and a maturity that can tolerate 'not knowing' for long periods.

The aptitude of engaging and experiencing symbolic communications provides an appreciation that life is both exclusive and inclusive, that life is singular to each individual and is within a context that is unimaginably greater. Over time, the ego becomes more curious about the unknown and is aware and more comfortable that an otherness lives through everyone and everything. An empirical learning occurs that there are subliminal currents which are beyond conscious understanding – and there is a growing sense of assurance and wonder in this way of living.

Like any relationship, there needs to be an openness to the other (the unconscious) and an understanding that this symbolic relationship is multifaceted, unpredictable and ever-changing. There may be times in a person's life when they require therapeutic expertise and support to find their way into this relationship and learn its language.

The shadow of individuation

> One does not become enlightened by imagining figures of light, but by making the darkness conscious.
>
> (Jung 1967, para. 335)

The term individuation is generally assumed to be associated with lightness, not darkness. However, there is a shadow side of individuation which can be an overidentification with the sublime whereby the ego is inflated by a 'call from the higher self'. The patient can delude themselves and use this 'spiritual call' as a justification for selfish and irresponsible behaviour, and when the therapist elevates their patient's story and colludes with their 'calling' under the guise of individuation, further destruction can occur.

A patient may want their 'calling' validated by a professional, and it is imperative the therapist considers whether their yearning to make a potentially life-changing decision is a result of a developmental life phase or an invitation to individuation. In the initial stages of therapy what looks like individuation can turn out to be a midlife crisis or vice versa, and there can be an overlap between the two. One way of discerning the difference and potential overlap is to support the patient to lean into their crisis (with safety considerations) and explore their options and the possible consequences. This exploration includes how their parents and other influential people reacted and lived with their desires and responsibilities. During the therapeutic process it can become clear whether the patient is struggling with a developmental transition of moving into another phase. This stage will include letting go and grieving who they thought they would be, or who they thought they needed to be, to be acceptable to themselves and others, or whether the crisis is a result of the pressures of individuation.

The case of Steven raised the question of whether his desire to set sail was individuation or a midlife crisis. The conclusion that it was primarily individuation was based on Steven's therapeutic exploration that included his ability to consider the impact and consequences of his behaviour. He understood his family of origin issues in this context and was able to mourn his adolescent fantasy of becoming an international yachtsman. He was also able to connect his grief with his underlying need to impress his father, as well as his need to compete with his father. Steven's decision was not reactive or impulsive; he had considered all options in depth and exhausted every scenario. There was no other way forward but to set sail, and he grieved in anticipation of how he thought those around him would react and the potential impact on their lives. He feared having to live with whatever the consequences were and could not imagine how the future would unfold if he proceeded. It was Steven's embodied psychological work that led to the conclusion that his process was one of individuation primarily, while acknowledging that his life stage would have made him more vulnerable to this process.

For some people individuation can be associated with an experience of numinosity, a feeling of 'coming home', or a deeply felt sense of connectedness. This experience is often kept private as a way of protecting its profundity and it can motivate a person to foster a relationship between their internal and external worlds, their ego and unconscious. This inner-outer relationship makes life increasingly rich and at the same time more challenging, as there is more attunement to relational and moral responsibilities.

How a therapist works is a reflection of their own individuation process

You yourself must be able to fulfil everything you expect of your patient.

(Jung 1973, p. 90)

This quote from Jung makes it clear that the therapist must ongoingly do their own psychological work. Failure to do so places the patient at risk of being unconsciously pressured to live out the therapist's unlived life. Alternatively, the therapist can unconsciously restrict their patient's individuation process to avoid feeling threatened by them. The therapist who provides one-to-one treatment is susceptible to isolation and loneliness and, because they are always the authority that sets the boundaries, they can get a false sense of their own importance. In addition, they may come to see the world only through a pathological or therapeutic lens or, depending on the presentation of their patients and the number of clinical hours they work, they may internalise a distorted perception of society and the people in it. All these distortions can erode the therapist's enthusiasm and lead them to question whether individual therapy can make any difference to the larger society.

This is the shadow of individual therapy, and it can be projected onto the patient and contaminate or derail their individuation process. This is why Jung is so emphatic that the therapist must work ongoingly with their own shadow and their own individuation process.

Conclusion

The individuation process includes grieving the fantasy of what we originally wanted to be, or who we thought we might be, after therapy. It is an arriving at one-self, having an inner contentment that is not compulsively driven to impress, emulate, recreate, imitate or pretend to be anything other than oneself. Living in this way places importance in tolerating the waiting, the wondering, and the questioning of what is known, and being open and curious about the emerging unknown. There is a seeking of authenticity and a desire to question and make meaning at both the everyday and existential levels of life.

References

Colman, W. (2006). 'Imagination and the imaginary', *Journal of Analytical Psychology*, 51(1), pp. 21–41.

Colman, W. (2010). 'Mourning and the symbolic process', *Journal of Analytical Psychology*, 55(2), pp. 275–297.

Dunne, C. (2012). *Carl Jung. Wounded healer of the soul*. London: Watkins Publishing.

Hauke, C. (2006). 'The unconscious: Personal and collective' in Papadopoulos, R. K. (ed.) *The handbook of Jungian psychology: Theory, practice and applications*. London: Routledge, pp. 54–74.

Huskinson, L. (2002). 'The self as violent other: The problem of defining the self', *Journal of Analytical Psychology,* 47(3), pp. 437–458.

Jung, C. G. (1934–9). *Nietzsche's Zarathurstra: Notes of the seminar given in 1934–1939.* Vols. I & II. Edited by Jarrett, J. L. London: Routledge.

Jung, C. G. (1966). *The collected works of C. G. Jung. Volume 7: Two essays in analytical psychology.* 2nd edn. Edited by Read, H., Fordham, M., & Adler, G. Translated by Hull, R. F. C. Princeton, NJ: Princeton University Press.

Jung, C. G. (1967). *The collected works of C. G. Jung. Volume 13: Alchemical studies.* 2nd edn. Edited by Read, H., Fordham, M., & Adler, G. Translated by Hull, R. F. C. Princeton, NJ: Princeton University Press.

Jung, C. G. (1970). *The collected works of C. G. Jung. Volume 11: Psychology and religion: West and East.* 2nd edn. Edited by Read, H., Fordham, M., & Adler, G. Translated by Hull, R. F. C. Princeton, NJ: Princeton University Press.

Jung, C. G. (1973). *C. G. Jung. Letters, volume 1: 1906–1950.* Edited by Adler, G. & Jaffe, A. Translated by Hull, R. F. C. London: Routledge.

Samuels, A. (1985). *Jung and the post-Jungians.* London: Routledge.

Samuels, A., Shorter, B., & Plaut, F. (1991). *A critical dictionary of Jungian analysis.* London: Routledge.

Stein, M. (2019). *Volume 1 of the collected writings of Murray Stein: Individuation.* Asheville, NC: Chiron.

Chapter 2

Challenges and constraints when working clinically with the narcissistic personality structure

Introduction

The personality structure of narcissism and the clinical treatment of this condition has been written about extensively in psychoanalytic literature, and in recent years the term narcissist is used generically in popular culture. Where I refer to narcissism, I am not talking about people with minor wounds that fit within contemporary societal labels. I am referring to people who are severely damaged and highly defended. Frequently, these people operate very well in the world – their outward performance is often socially and culturally revered, but it can be very much at odds with the primitive psychological state from which they function.

Taking the Greek myth of Narcissus as my starting point: the narcissist cannot turn their gaze inside. It is as if they have a deep, prohibiting, unconscious awareness that knows if they were to see their inner emptiness, they would not be able to go on with their pretend life. Consequently, the traits of a narcissist include strong and stubborn defences against an awareness of this inner emptiness, and this is why they must look outside to find an adoring other – as a compensation for this inner lack.

Narcissists need to protect themselves and others from seeing that they were unloved or conditionally loved, and therefore have an unlived inner and outer life. Daring to face this reality would also mean facing up to their emptiness, loneliness and depression. They would have to acknowledge that they were needed to fulfil a function for their parent or parents, not for who they were as an individual. In essence, they dare not face their experience of being loved conditionally, and their fear of being unlovable.

Otto Kernberg describes narcissists as presenting:

… an unusual degree of self-reference in their interactions with other people, and a great need to be loved and admired by others, and a curious apparent contradiction between a very inflated concept of themselves and an inordinate need for tribute from others. Their emotional life is shallow. They experience little empathy for the feelings of others, they obtain very little enjoyment from life other than from the tributes they receive from others or from their own

DOI: 10.4324/9781003558125-3

grandiose fantasies, and they feel restless and bored when external glitter wears off and no new sources feed their self regard.

(1970, p. 51)

Due to the narcissist being dependent on others to polish their socially adapted veneer, this expectation will also be placed on the therapist, and, if they do not meet these requirements, the therapeutic encounter will expose how they exploit the other to maintain their one-person reflective surface.

The narcissist's agenda is to 'look out' which is fundamentally at odds with the therapist's agenda, to 'look in'. This clash of agendas is the starting point for this chapter and will be theoretically grounded in Jungian, post-Jungian, and other psychoanalytic references. A metaphor will be used to provide another dimension for understanding the inner workings of the narcissist and the associated clinical challenges. The final section will explain how the process of individuation is con-textually placed in the treatment of narcissism.

'Looking out' versus 'looking in'

The psychological focal point of the narcissist is outside, and the therapist's is inside, which creates a disjuncture for the expected therapeutic outcomes. The therapist's agenda is for the patient to engage in their process of individuation and to do this, they need to look within, as reflected in the following quote by Jung: "… your vision will become clear only when you can look into your own heart. Without, everything seems discordant; only within does it coalesce into unity. Who looks out-side dreams; who looks inside awakes" (1973, p. 33).

My interpretation of Jung's quote is there is no clarity when we look outside as we are only dreaming. Our vision is clear when we look into our own heart; then and only then will we be awakened. This is the opposite of what the narcissist wants: they must look out and find the adoring other. Consequently, the therapist will be expected to play this role, and when they can understand how the narcissist was seen as a child, they can have insight as to why, as an adult, it feels so life-threatening for them to look within.

The child as a function for the other

For the sake of ease and consistency, I will refer to the primary caregiver as mother. Please bear in mind that narcissism is intergenerational: the child did not have a mother that supported their coming into being because she herself was not parented in a way that she could come into her own being. Given this context, narcissism develops when a child is not seen for who they are, but instead is used by a parent or parents, or caregiver, to fulfil a function (McWilliams 1994). This child is an appendage to the caregiver and is not seen as a separate individual.

According to Giles Clark, narcissism is formed when:

> … the parents make the most unfulfillable unconscious demand on the child/ infant, namely: 'Don't be yourself: be my unknown and unfulfilled needs. You are here to become my existence, my identity; you must not and do not exist for yourself.' They are, in effect, wanting the real child to go away, and as he/she grows up, so the more they will resent him/her, reject and abandon the emerging person.
>
> (1983, pp. 45–46)

The child does not know consciously they were used to fulfil a function, and the impact of this unconscious demand of the mother is that the child is not seen or understood. The consequence of not having one's own separate existence nurtured is that the child has a deep sense of shame, feels inherently faulty and unlovable. Another emotion that is characteristic of this maternal failure is chronic emptiness. Rushi Ledermann (1981) uses the analogy of a robot whose insides are hollow to describe the inner emptiness associated with narcissism. They believe that "[t]he lack of good internal objects brings about the feeling of hollowness and futility of the robot" (1981, p. 339). As a result of the maternal deficit, the child fails to internalise a positive-enough internal object and thus replaces healthy relatedness with power and control.

Donald Winnicott (1986) also refers to this core emptiness, observing that these individuals are then dependent on an invented structure and pseudo-ego to give them a sense of identity, and a method of quasi-functioning. Winnicott conceptualises this hollowness and invented pseudo-ego as 'the false self' and uses this term to refer to "… people who have unconsciously needed to organise a false-self front to cope with the world, this false front being a defence designed to protect the true self" (1986, p. 33). Due to the child's identity being borne of their functionality, it is questionable whether they can have any sense of themselves that is not diluted through their functional 'false self'. There is the hope that therapy will in some way facilitate the patient to have a sense of themselves that is somewhat connecting to a truer experience of themselves, but this will be dependent on the severity of the damage, the penetrability of the defensive system, and their capacity to engage in the therapeutic process. The narcissistic wound is buried and encapsulated and must never be revealed; they are never to be seen and must be defended at all costs.

Defending against the emptiness within

The defence system that the narcissist presents to the world is usually an impressive structure that contains well-established and sophisticated interpersonal manoeuvres that conceals their inner emptiness. The presentation of narcissism varies, ranging from being outwardly offensive and brash, to being self-deprecatingly timid and shy. The narcissist's physicality may have morphed throughout their development in a way that somatically reflects their defence system. They may use their physical attributes to provide an added boost when manipulating others to fulfil a function. Conversely, they may manipulate the other so they, the narcissist, performs a function for the other. Whatever way, healthy relatedness is replaced with dysfunctional relating.

The narcissist adamantly believes that everyone and everything in the world should (and will) do what they want. For them to be able to surge forward like this they must block out or distort reality. According to Warren Colman (2006), narcissists negate reality with the use of 'imaginary thought', also referred to as 'anti-symbolic thinking'; they believe that what is so in their fantasy is in fact reality. They cannot comprehend that their internal fantasy is not the same as external reality. The antithesis of imaginary thought is 'true imagination'. Colman writes, "... true imagination has a reality of its own that enhances our being in the world, the imaginary is a *misuse* of imagination, for the purpose of denying everything that opposes the subject's desire" (2006, p. 23). To engage in imaginary thought makes it impossible for the narcissist to entertain or consider a perspective other than their own; if they were able to use their true imagination, they could accept that everyone and everything in the world has different desires and schedules to them.

True imagination is also referred to as 'symbolic thought'. A person's capacity to symbolise includes an ability to communicate, put emotions into words and take the raw material of sensation, images, imaginings and stories and give language to them. When this involves another person there is an interplay of communicative digestion and processing, and an understanding of one's own mind while being open to, and curious about, another person's inner world and life.

Colman believes that imaginary thinking is indicative of an early loss that has not been mourned. The unmourned loss for the narcissist is a result of being unloved or conditionally loved, and engaging in anti-symbolic thought enables them to avert the recognition of the pain of this early loss. They are completely unaware of how this loss has impacted them as an adult and to what extent their life is still organised around this primitive wound. The only way this loss can be somewhat integrated is when

> ... what is wished for in fantasy and what is realizable in material reality can be accepted and mourned ... [t]he psychic reality of the internal world is thus dependent on the acknowledgement of it not being in the external world.
>
> (2006, pp. 33–34)

Knowing the unknown

If the unconscious loss is to be mourned it must be brought to consciousness, which occurs through understanding the relational quality between the baby and its mother. The integration of awareness and grief develops through the relational experience between therapist and patient. During treatment, the therapist will experience reactions when a patient's material activates their unconscious, referred to as the therapist's countertransference reactions, and the risk is that the therapist will unconsciously project these back onto their patient. The therapist must be attentive to these patterns and use them to gain insight into the patient's intersubjective landscapes.

Narcissism is an anti-relational, anti-symbolic state that cannot be spoken to from outside; it can only be worked with from the inside. It can be deeply disturbing for the therapist to be on the inside of this kind of defence system and experience the narcissist's deluded reality. However, the transferences and projections must be experienced, because the therapist's mind, body and countertransference provide essential information about the nature of the patient's narcissistic wound, and how their intergenerational system of narcissistic damage operates. The therapist must experience the system relationally and become 'infected', as this infection is the narcissist's channel of communication, and these communications deepen the understanding of what the therapist is working with. To quote Jung: "[i]t is inevitable that the doctor should be influenced to a certain extent and even that his nervous health should suffer" (1966, para. 358). The question that emerges when the therapist works within this kind of system is whether they are reinforcing the narcissistic defences by colluding with them or doing therapeutic work.

The Titanic, the narcissist

There are numerous stories told about the tragic maiden voyage of the luxury liner, the Titanic. I will offer two accounts and use creative licence to draw parallels between what happened to the Titanic and the manifestations of a particular presentation of narcissism, including the early developmental processes. The clinical challenges for the therapist will also be reflected upon in comparison to this disaster. These contemplations bring into clear focus the potentially catastrophic and sometimes deadly consequences for the narcissist, and for those around them.

The unsinkable narcissist

Built in Belfast in 1912, the Titanic was referred to as 'unsinkable'. It is sheer arrogance to think that a man-made structure could have that kind of immunity to nature. Similarly, nature is no threat to the narcissist who believes that their 'ship' cannot sink – their ideas, plans and creations are faultless. Instead, the narcissist believes they can triumph over nature and will recklessly and exploitatively do this to give themselves more kudos. There is a part in all of us that wants to defy nature especially in the face of sickness and death, but most individuals are aware of their human limitations and work within them. Not so the narcissist: for them, there is no healthy respect for limitations set by nature and other people.

The narcissist, or to continue the analogy, the captain, uses and views people as a functional extension of himself, which also applies to material objects such as, in this example, a ship. The narcissist merges with the person or object and appropriates its desirability in such a way that it becomes an extension of them. The captain wants what is outstanding, and so he fuses with the grand and splendid Titanic. He cannot see it as separate; it is an extension and reflection of himself, and he cannot admire and appreciate the ship for what it independently is.

The Titanic hit an iceberg four days out from Southampton heading to New York City. There were not enough lifeboats because the ship was considered unsinkable; furthermore, lifeboats would have detracted from the ship's elegant lines. The image of the ship, as assimilated by the captain, would be spoiled which, in turn, would spoil the captain's image because he and the ship are one. Aesthetics are so important to the captain they can override any rationality about the laws of physics. It is more important for the captain/narcissist to dazzle people with the splendour of their 'vessel' than be concerned about their safety and that of others.

The self-assuredness and confidence in the narcissist's presentation can be intoxicating and seductive – why would you question going on a journey with them? The captain wants passengers on the voyage for two reasons. Firstly, their role as passenger is to marvel at their glorious vessel, to continually inflate the captain's ego. If their ego deflates, they will experience the emptiness at their core. Secondly, the passenger is used as a function as the narcissist senses deep down inside themselves that their compass is faulty, and they need to appropriate the other's compass to keep themselves on track.

When the initial excitement of cruising on the boat subsides, and the passenger no longer needs to 'look out' with amazement, they will naturally want to 'look in' and share their experiences with another. However, the captain is simply not interested in the subjective experience of their passenger; they are not curious about others or anything that does not support their direction – and this includes icebergs.

The Titanic was a 52,000-tonne ship that collided with a 1.5-million-tonne iceberg, and nearly 1500 people died. Why did the captain refuse to comprehend the catastrophic risks? The need for immense recognition led the captain to ignore danger and natural limitations such as an iceberg 30-metres high. He was chaotically driven by the underlying pain of his early loss and the unconscious fear of being exposed as fraudulent and unlovable. The captain kept his traumatic history submerged by using imaginary thinking to negate reality, and the fantasy of the mass adulation upon arriving in New York in record time took precedence over the reality of an iceberg. As such, his thinking was anti-symbolic. If he had access to any level of true imagination, he would have been able to distinguish personal fantasy from reality, take notice of the maritime warnings and be honourably responsible for all the lives in his hands.

An observer witnesses the narcissist repeatedly hitting metaphorical icebergs. These can take the form of bankruptcy or monetary problems, mental and physical health issues, constant relationship breakdowns, affairs, divisive conflict amongst friends or work colleagues, and substance and process addictions. A narcissist can go on for years or decades continually colliding with icebergs, and it is astounding how they continue to persist despite the obvious destruction around them. An iceberg collision can also be considered subjective, because what the therapist sees as catastrophic may not necessarily be seen by the narcissist in this way. Or maybe the collision is catastrophic for the narcissist, but the secondary gains in the form of attention from others may far outweigh the stress of the catastrophe. They may use the sympathy the tragedy attracts as a way of redeeming themselves and acquiring others to appropriate to fend off their loneliness.

The aging process can also be extremely confronting for the narcissist who has used their physicality and swagger as weapons of influence, and, when these resources are not as effective or as accessible, the reality of the iceberg collision can be harder to defend against. Or the opposite can occur, in which the aging process is so frightening that extra defences are employed, and existing ones become further entrenched to deny this universal human phenomenon.

When an iceberg collision occurs, the narcissist's reaction may be one of intense emotion, and their anger and upset can give the impression they are finally getting in touch with their feelings. While they may be reacting to the sinking of their 'ship', it is not genuine grief. The therapist needs to discern whether they are reacting because their glorious structure has sunk, or whether they are responding to the tragedy they have caused. Their emotional response may be the beginning of an awareness that their life has been a fraudulent use of resources to hide behind. This indicates a capacity for symbolic thought as they can acknowledge their internal fantasy is different from external reality and is potentially an invitation or provocation to engage in the individuation process.

However, if a breakdown of the defence system occurs and the narcissist has accessible resources at hand in the form of finances and adoring others, they can resurrect their system or invent a new one. The narcissist can simply move onto another ship and remain oblivious to the destruction in their wake. There can only ever be one captain though, and when a narcissist cannot receive their own independent glory, the closest they can get to the upper deck is to be an appendage. In this way they can sit at the captain's table and receive all the benefits. They become a decoration with hidden intent: an unassuming presentation of narcissism.

The beautiful adornment, Echo

In the Narcissus myth, the 'other' was Echo. When the story begins, her character seems innocent and earnest as she observes and mirrors Narcissus, and delights in his exhibitionistic performance. On the surface, Echo appears to be exploited by Narcissus but looking more closely, Echo gains from her relationship with Narcissus and is a more subtle form of narcissism herself: she clothes herself in stories of being the victim and 'hard done by'. In contemporary society either gender can be in the Narcissus or Echo role, and within the relationship the roles can remain established or switch.

Please shine my surface

The following vignette is loosely based on the dynamics of the Narcissus and Echo myth and illustrates how Echo can present in therapy. Suzy was desperate to see a therapist because she had been dating a narcissist who had 'traumatised' her – he had callously ended the relationship without any 'real' reason. During the initial session she complained endlessly about his selfishness and presented a list of narcissistic traits and examples of how he met all the diagnostic criteria. Her focus was on convincing me that he was narcissistic, and she wanted me to provide a professional diagnosis so she could inform him of his personality disorder, and they could work through it together. Suzy was baffled when I questioned whether she had a role in the dynamic and responded with more examples to prove her point because clearly, I was missing something to have asked this question.

Suzy was a beautiful woman in her mid-forties. She attracted significantly younger men who were typically artistic, the last one being an actor who delighted in showing her off at his opening performances and industry events. However, like her countless other boyfriends, he ended the relationship with the same reason the others had given her – she was too old and did not want to have children. She felt utterly defeated from this recent break-up and wanted to return home to America after nearly 15 years in Australia. Suzy had no luck in finding an Australian man – she thought they would be different from Americans (i.e., they would not be narcissistic). There was also an obligation to her ageing parents who continually placed pressure on her to come home, as life was not the same without their only child. She relished the fact she could change her parents' mood and make them feel special.

The story that emerged in therapy was that her parents' decision to have a child was an attempt to relieve her father's depression and to give him a reason to live, as well as providing a sense of purpose for her mother. Suzy fulfilled a function for both parents: she was conditionally loved, and this dynamic was repeatedly enacted with younger men by being their adornment.

The following is an example of an interrelational dance between Echo (Suzy) and Narcissus (Tom, her younger boyfriend):

- Suzy tends to Tom by inflating his ego, which allows him to avoid his inner emptiness. By unconsciously fusing with him, she can (by proxy) take care of her own wound, which is to make a man feel special and alive, as she did for her father.
- Being fused with Tom means Suzy can remain unconscious of her own wound through tending to his. Although she would be surprised to see it, she is using Tom to remain unconscious of her own wound by focusing on and fusing with his. Furthermore, her wound is kept alive, but she does not have to tend to it – she does not need therapy because 'Tom has the problem'. Suzy does not have to be conscious that her inner life and relational world is arranged around her wound.
- This relational structure has a crucial asymmetry which means that it must inevitably fail. Suzy keeps her wound alive through avoidance; all her focus is on Tom. However, her relational aims are different to those of Tom. He wants a glamorous woman who will adore him and delight in his exhibitionistic

performance, and Suzy wants a man who will give up his 'freedom' and be 'tied' to her. As part of this contract he is supposed to be eternally grateful for her self-sacrificing adoration and endless mirroring of him.

- Tom is driven by his need to avoid his inner emptiness, and he has chosen Suzy on the basis that she does not want an authentic connection and only wants to make him feel special by inflating his ego.
- Suzy is left carrying both wounds. She is carrying her own wound through avoidance, because her focus is on Tom, and she is carrying Tom's wound, his inner emptiness that she distracts him from, by inflating his ego.
- The usual trajectory in this dynamic is for Tom to turn on Suzy, because he hates his dependence on her to maintain his avoidance of his wound. He fears his dependence may turn to vulnerability which will be exploited by Suzy.

Suzy became bored and tired of basking in Tom's success and good looks. When she began to question 'Where am I in this relationship?' death metaphorically entered the room. Tom ended the relationship because she was too old for him (narcissists often fear ageing and see it as contaminating). Upon this rejection Suzy regressed to a primitive, needy child and her pathology surfaced. She would either pout silently or rage hysterically and Tom saw her as a desperate, scary woman from whom he needed to escape.

For years Suzy deluded herself that the early stages of her relationships were true love. What she eventually came to realise was that she exploited her narcissistic wound in order to make a man feel special and alive. In therapy, Suzy understood this structure did not give her an opportunity to have a relationship with another person that was not largely based on pathological fusion or facilitation. When she started to date again, the important question Suzy asked herself was, 'What is this man protecting me from seeing in myself, and therefore having to live with in myself?'

The function of the therapist when working with these dynamics

There is a similarity between the role of the therapist and that of Echo: they both mirror and reflect positive regard. The concern for the therapist is whether the therapy is reinforcing the narcissist's defences by colluding with them and making them more entrenched, and more sophisticated.

When the therapist is a consistent and reliable presence who outwardly accepts their patient and weathers whatever emotional storms occur on a regular basis, the patient may get a false sense of themselves. They may think, 'if you can still be there for me regardless of how I treat you then I must be alright, and I can expect other people to put up with this behaviour as well'. The therapist's ability to tolerate a patient like this can reinforce the patient's delusions about who they are and can prevent them from seeking out other relationships in which they might be forced to confront their own reality. The risk of therapy can be that the patient internalises a normalisation of their narcissistic delusions and the therapy is the only long-term, sustaining relationship in their life. They can use the internalisation of this relationship as proof to themselves that they are functional.

Another consideration for the therapist is whether the patient's defences are becoming more sophisticated and more useable to exploit others. The narcissist takes something from someone without their permission (i.e., they appropriate) and this can be done to the therapist by impersonating and mimicking their psychological skills and capacities. It may appear they have made progress since commencing therapy because they seem to have developed 'emotional literacy' and have fewer outbursts. However, they have merely used the therapist to refine their socially adapted facade and have re-directed their explosions into the therapeutic relationship.

If the narcissist imitates the therapist's vocabulary and manner of enquiry it can be dangerous because ultimately it can increase their capacity for serious, sometimes life-threatening exploitation; for example, with narcissistic patients who have psychopathic pockets or addiction issues. When the narcissist develops a pseudo functioning that enables them to appear psychologically sound it can be extremely difficult to detect that their emotional intelligence is superficial, because it may be coupled with righteous conviction and seductive confidence. Narcissists can also use their experience of being in therapy to become therapists themselves. They can impersonate their therapist and duplicate this relationship onto their patients. Another version of this kind of appropriation can arise when the narcissist showcases their psychological intelligence in the arena of motivational speaking or a form of self-development. In both these examples the patient has not digested or integrated the theoretical framework and treatment they have received.

At the outset it may seem that the therapist is reinforcing the patient's narcissistic defences by colluding with them. However, they are knowingly doing this in the service of effecting change. Unlike Echo, the therapist has a separate mind. The therapist has a sensitivity to the patient's condition, and the clinical proficiency and knowledge that understands confronting or challenging too early may break rapport and prevent entry into the narcissistic defence system. The therapist must be inside this system and experience the relational quality of their patient's narcissistic wound to support them to mourn their unconscious loss.

The therapeutic encounter holds hope and the possibility of integration; however, this integration (or not) can be complex and hold deep pockets of darkness that cannot be predicted. It can be disturbing to be inside this system, and to be attacked and berated by the narcissist's arrogance and deluded reality. Also, the boredom can be almost intolerable. The therapist must be patient and open to experiencing their countertransference as it can provide essential information about the nature of the patient's wound and how their intergenerational system of narcissistic damage operates. As Jung says, "[y]ou can exert no influence if you are not susceptible to influence" (1966, para. 163).

The narcissist is anti-relational; they are not interested or curious about another's subjective experience, which is why it can be so hard for the therapist to stay awake. It is boring to be part of an audience that watches an endless, unchanging script, and when the main character cannot internally reference themselves in a way that leads to psychological or relational development, it is difficult to remain alert and engaged.

What the narcissist leaves in the room

There is another function the narcissist depends on the therapist for: to varying degrees, they know there is something disturbed and disturbing about them. This unspoken truth is often expressed through a suspicious glance or a dismissive platitude. They want this part of them to be seen and known, but they do not want to consciously process this; they want to deposit their disturbance and 'monstrousness' in the therapist and in the therapist's room, and leave it there. They must have an abode for this part of themself that can be known but not worked with. A patient who is structurally narcissistic has a bigger, hungrier and more desperate monster than that of a patient who has narcissistic traits. The therapist's room is used to house this monster which the patient wants to leave in their room forever and let the therapist process it for them; they do not want to take responsibility for it. Also, leaving this part of themself in the therapist's room means they can appear outwardly functional as they believe they are not carrying it with them. This monstrous gift that has been deposited by the narcissist is attached with exclusivity, and the therapist should feel grateful for being the recipient of this special love.

The therapist needs to be scrupulously honest with themself regarding their threshold of working with this style of patient; if not, they may unconsciously close down the opportunity for their patient to engage or continue in treatment. An example of this is when the therapist unconsciously confronts a patient before they are ready, and their brittle ego simply cannot endure what the therapist has offered. This break of rapport can be an unconscious expression that the therapist does not want to work with this level of narcissistic damage, or they have enough patients with this pathology and do not want another one, or they do not understand the extent of this damage or pathology.

The vicarious use of the patient

Narcissists can be divisive: some therapists can countertransferentially experience them as abhorrent while others may see beyond their bolshiness and are sympathetic. They are vulnerable to being used to fulfil a function for the therapist, just as they were used by their parents. The communications of narcissistic patients can overwhelm the therapist to the point where they lose their therapeutic composure. In an attempt to hold onto their separate mind, the therapist can covertly punish their patient by drifting into righteous fantasies of their patient's empty life and feel smugly pleased that they have such disturbing pathology. These patients can aggravate the therapist and push them to react in a way that is completely foreign to them and is not aligned with their ethics.

When a therapist does not take professional responsibility there is a risk that they will make vicarious use of their patients. These patients can become a ritualised frustration valve for thoughts and feelings that the therapist is wanting to avoid in themselves or other relationships. In short, they can provide a focus for the therapist's free-floating irritability, resentment, self-righteousness and superiority. The therapist needs to be able to reflect on their reasons for working with this type of patient; if not, the patient may be used in the way they have been previously. They need to ask themself, "What projections is my patient carrying for me so I do not have to look at my own narcissism?" "Are they a regular and predictable outlet for my own unprocessed and unintegrated emotions – both historical emotions and emotions that arise on a day-to-day, week-to-week basis?" This process of using another to hide our own shadow is described by Robert Johnson when he writes, "Jung used to say that we can be grateful for our enemies, for their darkness allows us to escape our own" (1991, p. 37).

In addition, the patient's need for the therapist to provide a reality check can offer the therapist a sense of false satisfaction and enable them to use their professional persona to hide their own anxieties about being valueless and useless. These patients can be seductive, famous, and powerful and this can elicit countertransferential excitement. There can be the initial hit of the honeymoon period and the early flush of fantasy that the therapist is the only one who can heal them, as the previous therapists have been grossly incompetent.

Due to the entrenched nature of narcissism, therapeutic progress is often slow and patients can need long-term treatment. They are often wealthy as many hold jobs that are highly valued socially. Narcissists can be offensive and exhausting and because of this, they may have only few, if any, intimate relationships in their lives. Since they are dependent on others to fend off their own loneliness, they are prone to seeking out therapists. All these factors can render them susceptible to financial exploitation by the therapist.

Narcissistic attacks can be cruel and destabilising, and the therapist may find it impossible to remember that these defences are an attempt to preserve the vulnerable child that has been severely damaged. In these circumstances, the therapist must acknowledge the harsh reality that some people are born into situations and have experienced trauma that has caused irreparable damage. The therapist must understand that treatment cannot 'heal' or 'cure' certain structural damage, and while the Jungian tradition places importance on the teleology of the unconscious (Papadopolous 2006), the search for meaning can cause the therapist to overlook the impairment of the patient. Attempting to find a purpose when none exists can be a defence against reality and the therapist may be avoiding their own inability to come to terms with life and the limitations of therapy.

A responsible therapist needs to reflect on how their patients can be used to fulfil a function for themselves. This process is explained by Clark: "The 'wounded healer' actually heals through his/her survival, management and recycling of his/her own wounds and madness. This contains and processes the maddening wounds of the other" (2009, p. 95). The therapist must be accountable and committed to unencumbering their narcissistic investments in the therapeutic relationship. When this healthy disentanglement from the patient occurs, the therapist can offer another perspective and integrate their personal experience to provide information that will benefit themselves and their patient.

Creating a container for the possibility of change

The narcissist needs to know that the therapist will not leave them. They will test the therapist repeatedly to determine whether they have the robustness to survive the patient's pathology, which they know is within them but do not want to acknowledge. Envy is one of the determining characteristics of narcissism, and some patients will attack the therapist's capacity to symbolise purely because they cannot symbolise themselves. These patients enviously disregard or destroy the links the therapist makes, because even though they may be relevant or correct, the narcissist cannot tolerate the therapist doing something they cannot.

It can take years of work to build a strong enough 'therapeutic container', a metaphoric space that is safe and protective for both therapist and patient, for the narcissist to be challenged and for them to entertain that external reality is not an extension of their inner reality. The following sequence explains how the therapeutic relationship and container creates the potential for the narcissist to develop a symbolic function, and for the therapist to challenge them when appropriate.

- The patient encounters limitations through the ego-bruising processes of rupture and repair that occur when the therapist holds the frame.
- While the therapist does not challenge the patient directly to begin with, they should be tracking and reflecting on their own countertransferential use of their narcissistic patient.
- If the therapist does this reflective work, they offer a space for the patient to acknowledge and withdraw their projections.
- When the patient can do this, it opens the possibility of grieving their narcissistic wound.
- This grieving also entails letting go of a version of their life that was based on performing an allocated function for a parent, parents, or caregiver.
- Through this process the patient becomes able to see the other, not just their projection. This separation enables the patient to develop the capacity to imagine how their behaviour might affect the other.
- This shift also opens the possibility of the necessarily slow development of empathy, critical reflection, and moral discernment. In time, the patient becomes able to acknowledge and reflect on differences of opinion and ways of being in the world.
- When this process is successful the patient develops a capacity for symbolic thought. They can acknowledge that what they hoped for is lacking in reality and are able to mourn this loss.

The collapsed empire: a narcissistic performance or genuine grief?

A therapeutic frame needs to be established in the anticipation of an experience that may overwhelm the patient. When this overwhelm occurs, the narcissist's reaction may be one of intense emotion, and their anger and upset can give the impression they are finally getting in touch with their feelings. The therapist must discern whether they are reacting because their empire has collapsed, or whether they are responding to the awareness that their empire is merely a reflection of their wasted life. A distinction must be made as to what the patient is experiencing because the direction of treatment is dependent on this assessment.

If the patient is reacting to their collapsed empire, they may be realising that they have lost everything. They will be afraid of being alone and may no longer have the resources to keep the system of mirrors in place that bolsters their ego and makes their life run smoothly. A pseudo depression may occur, which is different to a genuine depression. The type of depression is evident in the therapist's countertransference response as they find themselves fulfilling the role of audience to the narcissist's seemingly important psychological development. The patient can furiously blame the therapist for their collapsed empire because the therapy has not done what it was supposed to do.

The alternate response is a dawning awareness that the narcissist's life has been a fraudulent use of resources to hide behind. This acknowledgement indicates a capacity to symbolise and, when this occurs, there is an inevitable depression that follows. This state is a result of the adjustment from a two-dimensional omnipotent fantasy to a three-dimensional relational life. Along with this is the grief that comes with a growing awareness of the narcissist's behaviours and how these have been annihilating to themselves and those around them. Ceasing or reducing these behaviours can make the patient painfully aware of the hollowness and emptiness they have defended against all their life.

There is the hope that the patient will come to know who they are beyond their defences and develop a sense of moral and relational responsibility. Through this, there is the potential for an invitation or provocation to engage in the individuation process. An attitude of individuation is when a person can acknowledge there are underlying currents that cannot be controlled by the conscious ego, and that the ego needs to live in relationship with these unconscious upwellings. The individuated person is curious and wants to understand how to navigate the atmospheric conditions that directly affect day-to-day functioning while respecting that the greater forces are unimaginably vast, unpredictable and mysterious.

The overlap of agendas

As described at the beginning of this chapter, the narcissist's agenda is to 'look out' which is at odds with the therapist's agenda to 'look in'. The narcissist's unconscious plea is to be seen and understood and for this to happen they want the therapist to 'look in' at them. In the therapeutic process they are 'seen' for who they are: they are desperately lonely, dependent on others, and envious of anyone who is independent. As their therapist, you can 'see' them and how they have constructed a protective system out of their early damage. They may hate you for seeing it and love you for seeing it. They may hate that you hold a part of their history that has revolved around cruelty and exploitation, and love that you have survived their criticisms and attacks. In therapy there is a recognition of them beyond their defences and, if you are without the need to exploit, you may have a more honest sighting of who your patient is.

Conclusion

Personally, I continue to work with such patients because of an actual experience I have had with most of them, sometimes only once. This has been a profound moment in which their narcissistic wound has manifested itself in the therapeutic relationship in an embodied way. This experience of the depth and dimensions of their unmet need is unforgettable and provides me with the stamina to renew my commitment to the work. In this moment it becomes painfully clear why they need to 'look out' and enlist such powerful defences: the pain of not doing so is too great for them. Often the sessions that follow this insight can be an attempt to spoil the shared moment, but it is that experience that carries me. I may waiver in enthusiasm but will continue to show up and stay loyal to my commitment to the therapeutic impulse which is to 'look in'.

It is humbling to have momentarily experienced this person beyond their defences. What astounds me is the complexity and resilience of the psyche's attempts to preserve the damaged child. I am also struck by the uniqueness of each person's defences, how differently they manifest, and how this becomes the script for their life, which can be traced back to their earliest experiences. As therapists we must remember that we can never really know what is going on inside another person, and this includes our patients. An individual's inner world is exclusively theirs and we may have the privilege of being enlisted for part of their journey of exploration but ultimately, we do not know what the outcome will be.

References

Clark, G. (1983). 'A black hole in psyche', *Harvest Journal,* 29, pp. 67–80.

Clark, G. (2009). 'The embodied countertransference and recycling the mad matter of symbolic equivalence' in Heuer, G. (ed.) *Sacral revolutions: Reflecting on the work of Andrew Samuels – Cutting edges in Psychoanalysis and Jungian Analysis.* London: Routledge, pp. 88–96.

Colman, W. (2006). 'Imagination and the imaginary', *Journal of Analytical Psychology,* 51(1), pp. 21–41.

Johnson, R. A. (1991). *Owning your own shadow: Understanding the dark side of the psyche.* New York: HarperCollins Publishers.

Jung, C. G. (1966). *The collected works of C. G. Jung. Volume 16: Practice of psychotherapy: Essays on the psychology of the transference and other subjects*. 2nd edn. Edited by Read, H., Fordham, M., & Adler, G. Translated by Hull, R. F. C. Princetown, NJ: Princeton University Press.

Jung, C. G. (1973). *C. G. Jung. Letters, volume 1: 1906–1950*. Edited by Adler, G. & Jaffe, A. Translated by Hull, R. F. C. London: Routledge.

Kernberg, O. F. (1970). 'Factors in the psychoanalytic treatment of narcissistic personalities', *Journal of the American Psychoanalytic Association*, 18(1), pp. 51–85.

Ledermann, R. (1981). 'The robot personality in narcissistic disorder', *Journal of Analytical Psychology*, 26(4), pp. 329–344.

McWilliams, N. (1994). *Psychoanalytic diagnosis: Understanding personality structure in the clinical process*. New York: The Guilford Press.

Papadopoulos, R. K. (ed.) (2006). *The handbook of Jungian psychology: Theory, practice and applications*. London: Routledge.

Winnicott, D. W. (1986). *Home is where we start from*. London: Penguin Books.

Chapter 3

Gender identity and interiority in a contemporary Jungian context

Introduction

Some people never question their gender identity or how they want to express it. They may have some wonderings about what it would be like to live as the opposite gender, or they may try to get into the mindset of the opposite gender to understand why they think, speak or behave the way they do. Alternatively, they may think about living another variation of the gender they were born with, such as a more feminine or masculine version of themselves. Overall, these wonderings do not induce considerable distress and are often curious fantasies.

In contrast, the people I am focusing on in this chapter are those whose experience of gender identity does induce significant distress, that can at times be life-threatening. For example, some of these patients have described themselves to me as unnatural and that they should have never been born. These individuals are anguished and seek treatment because it is their last option to soothe a torment that has resulted in states such as depression and suicidality.

My work in this area is with patients who have been referred to me by colleagues who have seen them for several assessment sessions and have concluded that their gender identity issues are not a matter of them needing support with living as their preferred gender. Instead, there is a question of whether their gender-related issues are a manifestation of a personality disorder. Consequently, these referrals are based on the understanding that I will work with the patient's relationship with their body, gender and sexuality, and help them find their own understanding of the discrepancy (or not, as the case may be), between the reality and limitations of their desired expression of themself and the extent to which this aligns with their fantasy image of themself.

Central to this perspective is the awareness that patients can live with the fantasy that their life would be more satisfying and successful if they were the opposite gender or a variation of their masculinity or femininity. They can idealise the other gender or a variation of it because they cannot live comfortably in their own body, and they see the 'other' as not having the issues they associate with the biological configuration with which they were born.

Our body is the living history of our lives, and this can include issues that we do not want to remember or address. In such cases it is only natural that we do not want

DOI: 10.4324/9781003558125-4

to see the physical, visual evidence of our history, nor our personal and intergenerational history, because our body may be a painful, perhaps unbearable, reminder of something that we want to forget. My therapeutic role is to help the patient unearth their unconscious beliefs, such as if their body or gender were arranged in accord with their fantasy image then all their life problems would be resolved.

Background ideas and experiences

Some people choose to not be identified with a gender or sexual orientation or be placed on any spectrum, but for the sake of ease and consistency I will not be referring specifically to these people throughout this chapter. Nonetheless, the general principles discussed may be applied to them. Gender identity can be considered as a spectrum of positions, at one end masculine and the other feminine. Sexuality or sexual orientation is also on a spectrum, at one end heterosexual and the other homosexual. Gender identity and sexual orientation are separate spectrums. However, in life the expression of these aspects of oneself may overlap to a greater or lesser extent.

Both gender identity and sexual orientation are to varying degrees fluid, meaning that we can move on these spectrums. Some people's experience of these aspects of identity and interiority remain fixed throughout their life, and for others, these aspects can change once or more during their lifetime. Sometimes a person is comfortable with this fluidity, is conscious of it, and may actively enjoy it; sometimes it can come as a complete surprise. An example is a person whose long-term relationship comes to an end, and they find themselves drawn to a person who does not fit with their previous pattern of attraction.

There are many factors that can influence how stable or fluid a person's experience of their gender identity and sexual orientation is. These factors can include their chronological age, developmental life phase, who and what type of relationship/s they have been involved in, social and cultural encumbrances, physical and mental health issues (including history of trauma), access and availability of diverse experiences, process or substance addictions, medical issues and medication, and life circumstances and responsibilities. A determining factor is where a person is in their psychological development. Their gender identity or sexual orientation could largely be a repetition of unintegrated historic material, or it could be highly authentic, or it may be a combination of the two.

It is important to note that some people are born knowing what gender they identify with and that their physical body does not reflect their psychological gender. They have clarity in knowing their gender identity and how they want to express it. Obviously, these individuals may experience differing intensities of psychological and physical discomfort, but if they have meaningful support in their relationships, access to accepting services, available medical and mental health treatment, and adequate finances, they may live their desired identity with fluctuating degrees of ease and satisfaction. To reiterate, these people are not the focus of this chapter.

First vignette – Sam

Sam confidently identified as transgender and was determined to change his appearance to reflect his internal experience that was predominantly feminine. However, despite his certainty and expressed longing, he was unable to take any steps towards his desired outcome, which was why he was referred to me. My colleague tentatively assessed him as being transgender and was concerned that he had become depressed because of his inability to make any progress regarding his preferred gender identity. Another concern was his stubborn resistance to talking about himself aside from anything that was trans-related.

When I spoke to Sam on the phone before our initial appointment, I asked him what pronouns he preferred and he responded 'he/him'. The reason he gave was that he had not officially transitioned yet. I suggested that if this was to ever change would he please let me know. Consequently, when referring to Sam I will use these pronouns. During the session Sam was extremely awkward, his conversation was stilted, and the look on his face when he made eye contact was one of excruciating embarrassment. My countertransference towards Sam was a feeling of warmth and wanting him to know that I accepted him for the person he was. Over a number of sessions I came to understand that my positive countertransference was compensatory (Racker, cited in McWilliams 1994). I wanted to give him what his mother had not, which was unburdened interest that did not have the agenda of Sam being emotionally fused. I wanted to facilitate Sam's experience of being emotionally separate.

Sam was a 20-year-old only child who lived with his biological parents; his two half-brothers from his father's first marriage would only visit on festive events such as birthdays and Christmas. When Sam was at home, he compulsively played video games which did not appear to affect his exceptional academic success. His physical appearance was more on the masculine side of the spectrum due to his body structure and clothes. He had a small group of friends that he had gone to school with, but it was always Sam who would initiate contact with them. He felt they only included him in their outings because they would feel bad if he was to ever kill himself.

I was unsure why Sam continued to attend sessions as they seemed torturous for him, I could not imagine how he would think the benefit of therapy would override his uncomfortable experience. My concern was that his attendance was a repetition of the scrutiny and emotional distress that he experienced from his parents. However, he was adamant he wanted to continue in-person therapy despite travelling over an hour each way. After three months of working together, I started to feel frustrated that he would not express himself, which was a welcome relief from my previous positive countertransference.

The following six reflections from my clinical experience need to be considered when working with patients like Sam, and the upcoming case example of Paul, and in general when working with patients' gender identity and sexual orientation.

Should labels, theories and diagnoses be used?

On appearance, labels can serve to pathologise and medicalise, but for the individual they may be a source of comfort and identification. The patient can use labels or diagnoses to explore and understand their gender-related issues, experiences and questions. They may feel a label gives a name to and normalises their set of symptoms and are reassured that their emotions have been experienced by many others and that these symptoms are taken sufficiently seriously to be medically documented. Being able to identify as transgender or whatever term someone chooses to use may be extremely soothing and relieving for them.

The use of socially condoned and appropriate terms changes rapidly which can make it difficult to keep up to date and abreast of what is non-offensive. It is important to use what terms a patient identifies with as this enables them to connect more fully with who they are in the sessions, and if there is any doubt it is better to ask the patient what they prefer as opposed to attempting to build rapport by using an assumed politically correct term. Saying that, there is the hope that if the therapist has a disposition of openness and curiosity, this will prevail, not whether the term they use is politically correct or socially redundant.

For example, I had a patient who, for a long time, did not want to be referred to by a name, so I would simply say 'Hello'. In any written correspondence they would use an emoji of a blue and yellow fish to indicate it was from them. This was someone for whom the whole question of gender identity and names was too confronting and could not be addressed directly for some time.

As much as labels and diagnoses can be a source of comfort and identification, they can also be used as a defence. This was the case with Sam who did identify as being transgender – he had no doubt his psychological interiority was feminine, and his physical exteriority was masculine. However, Sam's inability to move towards transitioning was unexplainable, particularly as he had his parents' full support.

Sam read the book *Cruising Utopia: The Then and There of Queer Futurity*, written by Jose Esteban Munoz in 2009, which he referred to as fundamentally life changing. This book ignited Sam's identification with being transgender and was followed by internet research and joining online chat groups. For the first time in his life Sam had a group of friends (albeit online) by whom he felt accepted and they were his first experience of people wanting to initiate and continue communication with him. He felt liberated that he finally had the social validation he had always longed for. Sam was able to identify with his online collective, as he also experienced the symptoms of gender dysphoria and the associated feelings of depression, isolation, disenfranchisement, suicidal ideation and being misunderstood. He was utterly relieved that he not only had a diagnosis for his condition, but a group of people with whom he could share this.

After nearly a year of therapy, Sam slowly and painfully acknowledged a dev-astating truth: he came to realise that his resistance to transitioning was because he was not actually transgender. Sam came to understand that he identified with the emotional symptoms of gender dysphoria because they facilitated communi-cation with his group of friends. Sam's inclusion in this group had provided him with a bond that compensated for his lack of interpersonal skills, social unease and awkwardness. He connected with members of this group through perceived shared life experiences.

As Sam became aware that he was not transgender he experienced intense grief. He was faced with the reality that he struggled interpersonally and could barely articulate his authentic emotions, as well as not knowing what his gender identity or sexual orientation was. This was the turning point in Sam's process of under-standing himself with greater psychological depth, freeing him up from his previ-ous need to use labels and diagnoses as a defence.

The therapist can also use a diagnosis as a defence because they cannot bear the 'not knowing'. They may feel they are out of their level of expertise. Or they may have a lack of integrated awareness of their own gender identity or sexual orienta-tion and, as a result, move too quickly into cognitive fact finding. For example, the therapist may start questioning with an intent to determine whether the patient is transgender or not, who they have and have not told, whether they should or should not have surgery, what the effect is on their life. Such interventions may be inappropriate and break rapport because of the therapist's inability to tolerate the unknown in the room and their unknowing. It is crucial that the therapist does not intervene out of their own anxiety, or the pressure of wanting to give their patient value for money, or more problematically out of wanting to prove that they are an intelligent authority.

Gender identity and sexual orientation can be entangled with a personality disorder

A person who is intrinsically personality disordered can express their traits through their gender identity or sexual orientation. Or the opposite of this is when a person's authentic gender identity or sexual orientation is disenfranchised and is expressed as traits of a personality disorder. It is important that the therapist considers both possibilities. The focus of treatment may be on the personality disorder or support-ing the patient to express themselves more authentically and work with their inter-nal and external disenfranchisement. The expression of these parts of the patient may not be clear in the early stages of treatment and the therapist needs to hold in mind both hypotheses until a position becomes clear.

From the first perspective, the personality disorder is primary, and gender iden-tity and sexuality are an expression of this disorder. An example of this would be an adult man who, as a baby, did not experience sufficient 'primary maternal pre-occupation', that is, did not have a mother who adapted enough to his individual infantile needs (Winnicott 1986). As a result of this deficit, he unconsciously avoids engaging with a woman for any length of time to prevent the eruption of primitive emotions. In relationships he refuses to commit to one person and instead has multiple casual partners. He also expresses himself sexually by obsessively watching pornography that enables him to have control over how long he engages with the object of his visual desire.

An opposing perspective is the presentation of personality-disordered traits that are a defence against an authentic self whose gender identity or sexual orientation is unacceptable. This individual cannot live comfortably or acknowledge the authenticity of their gender and sexuality for fear of disenfranchisement from themselves, family or community. In certain societies and cultures these parts of themselves may render them liable to imprisonment and death. An example of this is a long-term married woman and mother who denies her desire to explore her attraction to other men and women. She seeks a new therapist every time she starts to connect with her feelings, and criticises and berates the therapist for not helping rid herself of these emotions. This attack on the therapist is a diversion from her own process.

Both perspectives can be related to my work with Sam. Based on his account, he was intrinsically transgendered and could not come to terms with living as a woman, and his interpersonal awkwardness, depression and suicidality were a consequence of this. What was discovered in his psychological exploration was his unconscious need to overidentify with the symptoms of being transgender in order to give himself a sense of self. Sam's symptoms were not an expression of him – they were him. By living through his symptoms, Sam did not have to engage with or explore any of the deeper issues that were underlying his questioning of gender and sexuality, or his interpersonal issues.

Sam's parents did not give him physical or emotional space, particularly his mother, who would go into his room and fossick through his belongings and his computer to find information about him. When his parents had their suspicions confirmed that he was questioning his gender identity by reading his online correspondence, they swiftly joined a support group and became role model parents for transgendered children. For Sam's parents, their son's questioning of his gender identity gave them an amulet to ward off their concerns that their son did not want to communicate with them. It absolved them of their inability to reflect on their historical shortcomings as parents. Their son was transgender so therefore this label exonerated them from their parental failings.

Sam described his parents as thinking and behaving as though Sam was an extension of them. He had no psychological freedom to develop a sense of self that did not involve his parents' conscious and unconscious expectations. This was why he did not speak in sessions: to do so placed him at risk of being taken over by the other. He experienced sharing information about himself as a loss of what was exclusively his, and so he worked hard to hold on to these vital and precious parts of himself. The turning point for our work was when I realised that for Sam to expose information about himself, was for him to lose himself.

In the sessions it was evident that Sam needed to be the one who initiated, and I would respond. Through many iterations of this cycle and noting the transference and countertransference dynamics, I was able to build some provisional models about how Sam's inner world and capacity to relate were structured. I knew progress had been made because, over time, he initiated more freely and enthusiastically. It was the lengthening of eye contact that indicated his increasing ability to contain himself and not fragment in the face of another.

I considered the therapeutic work with Sam as a preliminary step towards individuation. Sam was able to entertain that his myopic focus on being transgender was a defence against his relationship with his parents. Once he was able to acknowledge this, he began to separate what his version and expression of gender identity and sexual orientation meant for *him*. This work strengthened Sam's ego and capacity to symbolise and led to individuation.

Keeping an open mind on what position the patient is leaning towards

As described earlier, 'position' refers to either the personality disorder being primary and expressed through gender identity or sexual orientation, or the presentation of personality-disordered traits that are a defence against a self whose gender identity or sexual orientation opposes what they consciously or unconsciously want but cannot bear to acknowledge. The therapeutic encounter can reveal what position the patient is leaning towards, but, even then, the position may be fluid and remain so. The therapist must suspend their opinions to avoid foreclosing therapeutic exploration.

Second vignette – Paul

Paul was a 53-year-old biological man who was experiencing gender dysphoria. He functioned outside the home in a stereotypical masculine way: he was employed in the building industry, avidly watched football, and was the father of twins who attended university. At least once a week when he was inside the home, he not only wanted to dress as a woman, he *needed* to dress as a woman – as this change of gender expression somewhat relieved his dysphoria. Paul's dual gender expression created disharmony with his wife: she tolerated what he needed to do to relieve himself, but it was tormenting for her. She found his gender expression unbearable because living with this part of him was a constant reminder of the loss of her husband, the man she thought she knew. Paul's ongoing fear of losing his marriage and children led him to disown his feminine expression (whom he referred to as Lacy) by drowning her out with alcohol when he was at home. After five years of heavy consumption, he deemed himself an alcoholic and attended a structured programme to remain abstinent. The concealment of Lacy as well as the suppression of his sexual fantasies about men were displaced onto daily sobriety meetings.

These groups gave him a purpose as he was able to be of service to other members and support many people to move from living in alcoholic oblivion to abstinence.

The predictability that had defined Paul's life since sobriety took an unexpected turn when he received communication from a woman who claimed to be his half-sister, and had been adopted out. He refused to believe her until she sent a photo of herself and, when he saw it, he could not deny the similarity to his mother. After many sleepless nights Paul chose to do a DNA test, and the results proved that this woman was in fact his half-sister. This information changed the trajectory of Paul's therapeutic work. He began exploring his early relationship with his mother that he had previously shut down with euphemistic responses such as, "She did the best she could at the time". Paul's view of his childhood was relentlessly positive and he would attempt to entertain me with stories that always gave the sunny side up. There was one account from when he was a toddler that would not leave my mind: Paul was staying at his grandmother's house and, when undressing him for a bath, she laughed hysterically because he was wearing 'girly undies'. His grandmother used this incident as a source of ridicule towards Paul and his mother.

Paul was instantly likeable, with an affable manner. He would try to get a sense of who I was by engaging with me about the weather and asking questions regarding my personal life. Paul never appeared disgruntled by my refusal to disclose information, but I knew he was searching for something about me to use as a point of departure from which to talk about himself. His ongoing disorientation from my lack of self-disclosure and the discovery of his half-sister placed pressure on his defences, and the extent to which he needed to be the mirror for the other became apparent.

As therapy progressed Paul gained further insight into his desperate need to be of service to others and function as a mirror for them, just as he had for his mother. Paul's mother could not see him for who he was; she could only see him through her lens of unresolved grief regarding the girl she had adopted out. Her 'gaze' was a boy/girl muddle. For Paul to bond with his mother he needed to be of use to her and he made an unconscious pact to carry her grief, which translated in adulthood as: "In order to connect I need to please others, to not experience or show my authentic emotions, but to be jolly and take away and carry their pain". Paul's defensive manoeuvre of becoming a mirror for others became his 'false self', and this consequently thwarted the development of an independent sense of self (Winnicott 1986).

The question I held in my mind was: is he suppressing Lacy because his wife wants him to be Paul?

Individuation, connecting with Paul or connecting with Lacy

The opportunity for individuation when working with Paul was to remain curious as to whether: (a) his mother's unresolved grief impaired his authentic expression of his gender identity, which was Lacy; or (b) his deep wound was a result of not being seen disabled his capacity to develop an independent sense of self. These configurations were not understood or processed; instead, they were unconsciously embedded and expressed as shameful confusions of gender identity and sexual orientation. There is the hope that once he unearths and processes this material he can live as authentically as possible and these aspects of himself will be an authentic expression of who he is, as opposed to a source of distress.

The therapy moved between these configurations, and the psychological exploration and associated grief provoked Paul's engagement with his process of individuation. He had to tolerate not knowing what set of wonderings he wanted to live with, and knew that if he made a decision, it would be because he could not bear the unknown. At certain points in the treatment there can be countertransferential pressure to know 'the truth' about the patient's gender or sexuality. The pressure to be 'the one who knows' in this way can be immense and can cause a collapse of the boundaries within the therapeutic container, for instance, through self-disclosure.

Self-disclosure in the therapeutic container

One of my patients made the following statement, couched as a question, "I assume you have a trans history?" If I did disclose whether I was transgendered or not I would have foreclosed their exploration and robbed them of an opportunity to explore their assumptions and projections about the other, and ultimately what these communications say about themselves. When the therapist discloses details about themself it enables the patient to start shaping their responses around what they assume the therapist will approve of. This curating of themselves around what they believe the therapist wants can ultimately reinforce their defences and create a further confusion and dysphoria.

Parents always have an unconscious or conscious gender or sexuality preference for their child, and the ramifications and complexities of these expectations can greatly impact the expression of both these areas in their children. In the transference there is the likelihood that the patient will want to know the therapist's preference for their gender identity and sexual orientation because they want to please, impress or reject the therapist, and potentially reenact what occurred with their parental figures. Most patients want to be accepted for who they are and self-disclosure from the therapist (even an attempt to prove their political correctness or to soothe) can obstruct necessary exploration of what needs to be processed and understood.

How the therapist can vicariously use their patient

Gender identity and sexual orientation can be areas of curiosity, fascination, disapproval and disgust that offer the therapist an opportunity to use their patient's life as a source of vicarious erotic stimulation. When the patient shares their material, this reporting of their life can stimulate an unintegrated pocket of desire or disgust (often sexual) that may be an area of interiority the therapist has not explored in their own personal life or therapy. The therapist may be uncomfortable about their countertransference reactions and be unwilling to take these to supervision. Often such a pocket of erotic charge is different from, or at odds with, the therapist's gender identity or sexual orientation.

If the therapist has not worked with these aspects of themselves, there is the risk that they will live them out vicariously through their patients. When this happens, the therapist is placing pressure on the patient to live out their own unlived fantasies and curiosities, and the patient can become a ritualised frustration valve for the unconscious and unexpressed gender and sexuality issues of the therapist. The therapist is tending to themselves, not their patient, and they are impeding the work their patient needs to do.

Conclusion

The expression of gender identity and sexual orientation are aspects of oneself that can be problematic and, for some, crippling. However, if these areas are worked with therapeutically there may be an opportunity to engage in the individuation process. The therapist must consider if the patient's presentation of personality-disordered traits is a defence against a self whose gender identity or sexual orientation opposes what they consciously or unconsciously want, or if the patient's personality disorder is expressed through gender identity and sexuality. It is crucial that the therapist resists the impulse to take a position, and instead remains open to both configurations to facilitate the emergence of material that ultimately can be an invitation or provocation to the patient's individuation.

Also, the therapist must consider the patient's developmental history, life experiences, and circumstances, and be attuned to the relational dynamics in the room. Gender and sexuality are complex, unsettling and ambiguous, and the exploration of these areas requires the therapist be vigilant and reflect frequently on their own defences and investments. They must remember a patient's gender and sexuality are exclusively theirs and the therapist cannot assume any ownership or authority on this private, sensitive and dynamic relationship with oneself.

References

McWilliams, N. (1994). *Psychoanalytic diagnosis: Understanding personality structure in the clinical process.* New York: The Guilford Press.

Munoz, J. E. (2009). *Cruising utopia: The then and there of queer futurity.* New York: New York University Press.

Winnicott, D. W. (1986). *Home is where we start from.* London: Penguin Books.

Chapter 4

Clinical and spiritual perspectives on the interrelational dance of addiction, compulsion and obsession

Introduction

The intention of this chapter is to offer reference points to therapists when they are working with patients who are experiencing addictive patterns and processes, and for them to discern when their patient's quest for spirituality is inauthentic or distorted by an existing pathology. My perspectives are largely based on 17 years of experience in the 'Alcohol and Other Drugs' department within a maximum-security institutional setting, and more recently with patients in private practice.

There are a number of treatment options and paradigms of interventions that are available in the community and privately for patients to address their addictive processes. Every treatment option (including private therapy, on which I will be focusing) has advantages and disadvantages, and the factors that need to be considered for the choice of treatment include:

- the substance or process being used;
- the duration of use;
- the intergenerational history and pattern of use within the familial system;
- previous treatment interventions;
- psychosocial factors;
- cultural factors;
- prescribed medication;
- physical health;
- mental health; and
- motivation of the patient.

These are all factors that must be assessed to determine the best possible treatment option for the patient, bearing in mind that what can be highly beneficial for someone when they first abstain from use may not necessarily be the most effective option post-abstinence. All treatment options have their place; it really depends on the individual's needs at each particular stage in their journey. What matters is how the different treatments and paradigms can complement each other in the service of the patient. Also important is the therapist's capacity to determine the

DOI: 10.4324/9781003558125-5

appropriate option, and then continue (or not) to work with their patient for them to receive the complementary benefits of the modalities they are engaging with.

A personality disorder can be masked by an addiction and unless the patient is willing to undertake their own process of individuation, the addiction will continue to shape-shift, attaching itself to different substances, people or processes. Meanwhile, the underlying personality disorder remains untreated. Individuation begins when the ego ceases to identify solely with consciousness and, instead, the ego becomes a mediator between conscious and unconscious aspects of the psyche. Through this process the person can come to know something of who they are at a deeper level, both particular and universal (Jung 1971).

An addiction can continue long after the actual consumption of the substance, or enactment of the process (e.g., screen use) stops. Even when the person has not used their substance or process of choice for an extended period, they can either be preoccupied with the effects of it or divert this obsessive attention or compulsive behaviour onto something or someone else. Addictions can indicate an underlying pathology that must be worked with to enable the individuation process. Within this framework, this chapter is divided into eight parts, and are summarised as follows:

1   *The difference between obsession, compulsion and addiction*

An obsession or compulsion can continue independently, long after an addictive process has ceased. When this occurs the addiction has 'morphed' and can be active in compulsivity that finds something else or someone else to attach itself to. Addiction can also morph into and remain alive as obsessive thoughts which are a form of repetition compulsion. In this way, the patient endlessly repeats a reconstructed version of the original addictive cycle in their mind as a way of trying to gain control over it. This pattern can remain unchallenged despite abstinence from their substance or process of choice because what was previously enacted externally is now enacted internally in fantasy. I discuss my work with Chloe to demonstrate the dance between addiction, obsession and compulsion, how each one of these three elements can take the lead at a certain time, and how they can work together.

2   *One addiction can replace another*

The exploration of obsession, compulsion and addiction and their interrelationship leads into a discussion of my work with Justin, who appeared to have completely turned his life around after stopping a 20-year habit that was subliminally endorsed by his father. His appearance was of someone who had achieved mind, body and spirit transformations. However, the underlying nature of his addiction was unchanged and showed itself as unintegrated displays of 'psychological awareness'.

3   *The quest or exploration of an altered state for meaning and purpose*

In this section, the same clinical examples of Chloe and Justin will be used to explore what is happening when a patient becomes 'over identified with the painful reality of suffering' and when someone 'escapes suffering through seeking freedom'. In the context of 'spirituality and the numinous', six questions and observations are suggested when considering whether a patient's individuation process is genuine or is being perverted or distorted by their addiction.

4   *Why individuals are 'drawn' to certain addictions*

Discussed here is the idea that an important unconscious function of a patient's addiction is to communicate pre-verbal losses or lacks in their early relationships. This unconscious communication also includes their 'choice' of substance or process. To illustrate this point, I return to my work with Chloe and describe how her ritualistic cycle mirrored her maternal relationship and how this manifested as projective identification during therapy.

5   *The pull of the addiction*

The patient wants to be free from their addiction but there can be a lot to lose by giving it up. For example, it can be a buffer against life, a way of coping, an identity or comfort associated with staying connected to a family system. It can also mean the loss of a pseudo-relationship that may be the closest and most reliable relationship the patient has ever known. Beyond these reasons is the possibility that an addiction can provide a framework which contains their madness.

6   *The relationship between an addiction and a personality disorder*

An addiction can mask a personality disorder, and this may become evident when the addiction ceases. When this is the case, treatment is not successful unless the disorder is recognised because the craziness of addiction can be vastly more bearable than the madness of a personality disorder.

7   *Spiritus contra spiritum*

Jung's use of the Latin phrase, *spiritus contra spiritum* (1976, p. 625) is the concept that a spiritual intervention is required for an alcoholic to recover. This observation can be understood as saying that, if they are to recover, patients need to seek a spiritual experience instead of looking for spirit in a bottle. This concept that patients need a spiritual intervention is, from my perspective, applicable to all patients with addictions. At the same time, addictions can be seen as a perversion of the spiritual quest and can indicate an underlying pathology that must be worked with to clear the way for an individuation process to occur.

8   *Can you work with addicts if you have never been an addict yourself?*

A discussion is presented here to consider whether a therapist can work with addicts if they have been an addict themselves, or alternatively if they have never been an addict, and what the ramifications are of either scenario.

Obsession and compulsion are often associated with addiction which is why I will start by discussing the relationship between them.

The difference between obsession, compulsion and addiction

Repetition is a defining feature in addiction, as it is in obsessions and compulsions. Obsessions are incessant, unwanted thoughts and compulsions are incessant, unwanted actions, and both are inherent in addictions (McWilliams 1994).

The person with an addiction is enslaved to a substance or process that leaves them in a state of craving and fixating on something or someone in order to experience certain sensations in their body and mind. What also comes with an addiction are short and long-term consequences, as well as concealed consequences that may not be apparent to the addict or those around them for years into their addictive cycle.

An addiction comprises an interrelational dance between obsessional thinking, compulsive action, and craving. Each one of these elements can take the lead at a certain time, or they can work together in unison. The rhythm of the dance is dependent on what stage of the addictive cycle the person is in.

First vignette – Chloe

Chloe was a 34-year-old woman who worked as an events coordinator. During the week people continually contacted her to discuss details of the upcoming social and corporate events she was organising. Chloe relished this role as it gave her some relief from her deep-seated fear of being alone, which she felt most intensely in the evenings when she arrived home after work. She would attempt to soothe herself with the anticipation of being around her friends on the weekend. However, her so-called friends were only enthusiastic about using cocaine and partying with her on Friday or Saturday nights – they had no interest in seeing her or 'hanging out' at any other times. Chloe could not understand why she was unable to sustain friendships and have a meaningful, intimate relationship. The relief she felt on weekends was only temporary, and the mid-week loneliness became so unbearable that eventually she sought therapy.

My countertransferential feelings towards Chloe were of disbelief, particularly at her stubborn refusal to acknowledge that her weekend binges were connected to her anxiety, relationship status or friendships. She would condone her drug use with elaborate justifications and refused to consider a perspective other than her own. Chloe would patronisingly explain how everyone her age used the substance, and that she would be alienating herself if she did not participate in this commonly shared activity. Also, given her fear and experience of loneliness, why wouldn't she engage in recreational drug use?

As therapy progressed, it became evident that her loneliness peaked when she scrolled through online social media after her friends had left. She would lie in bed and compulsively search for current posts of previous casual flings that never eventuated, and old friendship groups that did not invite her out anymore. This ritual was torturous for Chloe, as was the following day when she would obsessively ruminate on these images and attempt to conjure up narratives to explain why these relationships had failed.

Over time I noticed that my countertransference towards Chloe was split, and my reactions depended on whether she was talking about her addiction, her compulsivity or her obsessiveness. When she talked about her addiction I experienced frustration at her inability to acknowledge any consequences of her use. When she described her compulsive scrolling and obsessive thoughts post-cocaine use,

I wished she would stop her barrage of irrelevant details and tell me how she felt. Occasionally, the relentless description of past situations and people would cease, and she connected with her feelings and erupted with emotion. If this expression of emotion did not happen, the cognitive content would gain momentum and escalate into a frenzied state that stopped when I announced the session was ending. When this occurred, she was engulfed with feelings of rejection as she became aware that there was another person in the room, not just an audience.

I imagined it was Chloe's fear of loneliness and rejection that drove the addictive part of her to buy a bag of cocaine towards the end of the night. She would sense when her friends wanted to go home, and she needed to co-opt them into staying because she could not bear the emptiness when they left. After they had gone, Chloe would again torture herself, looking online to re-experience past rejections partly to access familiar feelings but also to prove to herself that she had mastery over her pain.

Even though Chloe's obsessive thinking was an attempt to not experience her feelings of emptiness and powerlessness, her obsessive-compulsive self still had more grasp on reality than the unformulated, raw emotional desperation which drove her to always get bags of cocaine at the end of the night. The point here is that a person is more capable of reality-testing when they can experience and reflect on their obsessiveness and compulsiveness than when their addiction has taken over. Once this occurs, they are less likely to be honest with themselves.

One day, Chloe became very unwell with influenza and was unable to partake in her weekend routine. She could not believe that none of her friends offered support but, more interestingly, she discovered that when they went out for dinner, they did not go back to anyone's house to use. During this four-week period of enforced abstinence, Chloe was able to acknowledge that to keep this group of friends and deepen the connection with them, she needed to stop being the one who instigated buying cocaine. With this realisation her weekly cocaine use abruptly stopped, and her obsessive thinking and compulsive behaviour found a new expression through online dating.

One addiction can replace another

The cessation of the substance or process addiction does not mean the person is not obsessively and compulsively preoccupied with what they are abstaining from. They may have simply diverted this frantic energy into something or someone else. The time that passes since detoxification and withdrawal, and duration of abstinence, is no indicator of whether they have truly addressed their addiction. It can only be said that they are in active recovery when the following three aspects of their addiction have been addressed:

- the underlying obsessiveness and compulsiveness which has driven their addiction;
- what their ritualised cycle has mirrored in their early relationships; and
- their desire for connection (often containing something spiritual in nature).

Once these factors have been tended to, the person may then have moments or periods of time in which they are able to function with a level of internal calm, as opposed to an ongoing battle for self-control.

Second vignette – Justin

Justin drank alcohol from the age of 14 with his friends on the weekends. When he got a plumber's apprenticeship with his father's company, his consumption increased to six days a week and he would drink beer with his father and fellow workers. This consumption of alcohol was entrenched in his routine: it not only marked the end of the working day, it was also a reward for successfully completing another day. Furthermore, it was an opportunity to please his father who often commented on how much he looked forward to these afternoon beers with his son. This time together was integral to Justin's experience of his relationship with his father, and it was an important part of Justin's father's own masculinity.

One Monday morning Justin and his father were on a job together and his father had a massive heart attack and later died in hospital. Justin was completely disorientated without the anchor of his father and their afternoon sessions which had grounded him. After the funeral he went on a two-day bender and was arrested for driving over the legal alcohol limit. The court ruled that Justin have a medically supervised detoxification administered by his general practitioner. This allowed him to keep his driver's licence provided he had regular, random breath tests with a zero-alcohol reading. Amidst all this, he was forced to step into his father's role and take over the business. Justin was relieved that he had to abstain from alcohol as the thought of drinking without his father was unbearably painful.

Justin was also mandated to attend a support group for alcoholics three times a week. He would attend the group after work and much to his surprise, enjoyed these meetings; but the source of his pleasure was the conceited contempt for his fellow attendees. I was perplexed that he did not seem to have genuine empathy for the other participants. By being able to listen to others and offer solutions he *appeared* to have compassion, but inwardly he pitied these people and his sympathy was condescending. He saw himself as superior and would use other members' narratives to showcase his ability to turn his life around seamlessly in a way they could not.

Justin's addiction to alcohol had ceased. However, what started to emerge was his obsessiveness and compulsiveness that had not been apparent when he was mindlessly going through the motions of life – working, drinking, weekends at the pub. Because he no longer drank with his fellow workers at the end of the day, he would compulsively fill every hour with activity. He attended his sobriety support group, went to the gym and, in the evenings, he would see his new girlfriend whom he met at one of his group sessions. They would talk at length about their recovery. The weekends were filled with activities relating to sobriety, exercising, or taking his girlfriend to his immediate and extended family events. Justin had a new identity: he was able to share his thoughts and feelings in a way he had not been able to before, and people marvelled at his apparent insight and capacity to self-reflect. Although he was just repeating what he heard at his group meetings, this new identity gave Justin kudos, compliments and attention.

Meanwhile his obsessiveness remained evident in his internal dialogue – he was constantly self-monitoring and hypervigilant about achieving mastery over his desire to drink. He would then externalise this urgent need to control into compulsive activity. This obsessive quality also manifested in his interpersonal communications when he was in any group or social situation; he was not at all present to what the other was saying or experiencing. Instead, he was constantly thinking about how he could insert his sobriety into the conversation and bring it back to himself in order to feed his ego and his own self-glory. As Freud explains:

> … the content of mania is no different from that of melancholia, that both disorders are wrestling with the same 'complex', but that probably in melancholia the ego has succumbed to the complex whereas in mania it has mastered it or pushed it aside.
>
> (1917, p. 254)

Seen in this light, Justin had a manic response to the cessation of his active alcoholism: he reinvented himself with a new identity as a self-proclaimed ex-alcoholic who had heroically defied the odds and turned his life around. Likewise, his response to the tragedy of witnessing his idealised father die in front of him was, as Freud (1917) describes, a manic response – Justin had pushed this loss aside with minimal mourning. This manic response was driven by a need for ever-greater control, and his co-dependent relationship with fellow ex-alcoholic provided another vehicle for his manic obsessive and compulsive thoughts and actions.

Justin appeared to have conquered his thoughts, emotions and behaviours, but in fact had learnt nothing from them. His 'triumph' was fragile – it depended on maintaining mastery over his own authentic feelings of vulnerability and never being at the mercy of his drinking or experiencing grief over the death of his father. This situation was inherently unstable as it was only a matter of time before these splits and defences started to fracture, as his unmourned and unknown grief continued to seek expression.

As can be seen from my work with Chloe and Justin, obsessiveness and compulsiveness are characteristically synonymous with addictive processes. However, there are many other traits and characteristics that are not only symptomatic of addiction but also can be seen as driving an addiction. In the rest of this chapter I will be exploring and explaining some of these other processes to give a broader understanding of the topic. Specifically, I consider our use of substances or processes in search of euphoria or the sublime as sometimes this is part of a longing for a spiritual quest or meaning. In the next point I will examine the relationship between addiction and these needs.

The quest or exploration of an altered state for meaning and purpose

At some stage in life, most people show an interest in investigating or at least considering spirituality or the transpersonal. This can come in many forms such as being intrigued by the possibility of inducing an altered state, a crusade to seek meaning, a pursuit for a purpose, a need to find a bigger perspective on the human condition, or aspects of all of these put together. It is important for therapists to be open minded and curious because the form of experiment(s) the patient has tried or is trying can speak to what they are internally and externally processing or needing to come to terms with.

The motivation or trigger to explore these can be:

- *developmental*; for example, mid-life;
- *circumstantial*; for example, a relationship break up or the death of a loved one; and
- *psychological*; for example, a need to explore a greater sense of belonging.

These motivations almost invariably arise in relation to matters of birth and death, mortality, loneliness, grief, spirituality, and a yearning or desperation for direction and meaning in life. They may also entail a working through of the patient's relationship to the religion or faith they grew up in. Joan Halifax explains:

[o]ur journey through life is one of peril and possibility – and sometimes both at once. How can we stand on the threshold between suffering and freedom and remain informed by both worlds? With our penchant for dualities, humans tend to identify either with the terrible truth of suffering or with freedom from suffering. But I believe that excluding any part of the larger landscape of our lives reduces the territory of our understanding.

(2018, p. 2)

This tendency to polarise to the extreme means that people can either:

- *Over identify* with the *painful reality of suffering* which results in distorted relationships with self and others, or
- Focus on *escaping suffering* through seeking freedom from the day-to-day.

An example of the first strategy would be someone who myopically focuses on the intricacies of life and is not open to something beyond their physical body that may give them comfort or be a source of inspiration or meaning. Their focus on the suffering aspect of the human condition can stir up a need for relief but, with no belief in anything greater than themselves, this can lead to egocentricity or consumerism. Looking at Justin's behaviour from this perspective we can see that, although he seemed to experience a spiritual shift in his life, he was still profoundly egocentric. He thought he was better than his fellow alcoholics and saw himself as an uninformed alcoholic who had transformed *himself* into an informed ex-alcoholic who could now save others by sharing his story and providing strategies. Even though the philosophy of his support group had a strong focus on spirituality, he did not live these beliefs in an embodied way. Instead of being a fellow traveller, an alcoholic among alcoholics, he preached the philosophy and used it to become the focus of attention.

The second strategy is the pursuit of freedom from suffering, that is, trying to flee from the reality of life's hardships. The decision to live in denial of the human condition and all the complexities that come with it can be either conscious or unconscious. An example of this is the person who does not take responsibility for their body and mind and recklessly seeks a distorted liberation using whatever substance or process they can to anaesthetise or alter their physiological and psychological state. This pattern can be evident when they are in the throes of addictive behaviour.

These two strategies can also work in unison. For example, Chloe was consumed with anguish on weekdays about whether she would be invited out by her group of friends at the weekend; or, if they were not meeting, she would frantically seek someone who would want to be with her on Friday or Saturday night. She would obsess over whether there were plans being made behind her back, constantly checking her phone for potential invitations. This obsessing was fuelled by the suffering that came from her conviction that she was about to be rejected and abandoned by her friends. She would then seek freedom from this suffering by using cocaine to manufacture an altered state that would give her a sense of pseudo-freedom, partly through the effects of the cocaine, and partly through the feeling of belonging. Her desperate need for this sense of belonging was what drove her as she tried to orchestrate her friends to gather around the cocaine that she had sourced.

Halifax questions, "[h]ow can we stand on the threshold between suffering and freedom and remain informed by both worlds?" (2018, p. 2). In other words, how can we live in the world and experience the multitude of emotions at a grassroots level while being open and curious to the forces that are greater than us, that can be known through dreams, imagery, myth, synchronicities and symbolism? A balance needs to be maintained – we need to straddle both worlds, and let each inform the other. If we are to experience our individuality on a day-to-day basis within the collective community, we need to foster this duality and be able to encounter a sense of meaning, purpose or comfort from something that is outside our cognitive comprehension.

Spirituality and the numinous

Some of the things that occur outside our cognitive awareness belong in the realm of spirituality. According to Christina Groff and Stanislav Groff:

> [t]he term *spirituality* should be reserved for situations that involve personal experiences of certain dimensions of reality that give one's life and existence in general a numinous quality. C. J. Jung used the word *numinous* to describe an experience that feels sacred, holy, or out of the ordinary.
>
> (1990, pp. 39–40)

As Murray Stein interprets Jung, a numinous experience is "… a hint that larger, non-egoic powers exist in the psyche, which need to be considered and ultimately made conscious" (2019, p. 53). Both quotes acknowledge the personal and transpersonal and the importance of there being an integration between the two. In Groff and Groff's quote, there is the experiencing of a certain dimension of reality that is grounded in existence, and in Stein's the numinous experience must be integrated into conscious awareness.

Jung describes how the numinous is experienced when he writes:

> … the *numinosum*, that is, a dynamic agency or effect is not caused by an arbitrary act of will. On the contrary, it seizes and controls the human subject, who is always rather its victim than its creator. The *numinosum* – whatever its cause may be – is an experience of the subject independent of his will … this experience as being due to a cause external to the individual. The *numinosum* is either a quality belonging to a visible object or the influence of an invisible presence that causes a peculiar alteration of consciousness.
>
> (1958, para. 6)

Crucially, the numinous experience *arises*: it is not created or induced on demand. Instead, the individual is overcome with the ferocity of the force of the numinous and is left with an altered consciousness which requires integration. For this to occur, an individual must have a strong-enough ego for the experience to be integrated, or, at least have a supportive therapeutic relationship in order to facilitate this process of integration. The patient must understand that the numinous experience is isolated and will never be repeated in the same way or form again. There must be a level of psychological maturity for the person to treasure this profound experience and respect that it cannot be repeated. Some people obsessively and compulsively try and recreate a numinous experience in a way that works against its likelihood of occurrence. However, a container can be put in place to open a space for the possibility of numinous experiences.

An individual can *pervert* or *distort* the true meaning of a numinous experience by placing a conscious or unconscious expectation and agenda onto it. They can blindside themselves by seeing the numinous as a romantically enticing, altered state that will provide answers and insights into their existential questions and emotional torments. A numinous experience can be falsely used to give direction in life, or quite simply anaesthetise oneself to the pressures of life. This practice of distorting the true meaning of a numinous experience can be symptomatic of an addiction.

The following questions and observations can be used to think about these dynamics clinically:

- Is the person *present* to what is occurring around them? Or are they checking out of life and solely feeding their ego at the expense of others and/or their situation?

- Have their experiences of an altered state satisfied them? Can they *stop,* while they still want more?
- Common to all addictions is the experience that, over time, the practice of the addiction results in diminishing satisfaction and a wanting more and more. This escalates, as do the associated consequences. The addicted person's experience is that the initial relief of the 'hit' gets hollowed out and the more they engage in the addictive cycle, the hollower it gets. As this occurs, what was enjoyable when their use started can turn into a bottomless well of self-hatred with shame and fear.
- Does the person have an *expectation* attached to what they want to induce or experience through their use? If so, this premeditated or contrived agenda becomes the focus of conscious experience instead of being open to any authentic transpersonal experience which might arise. For example, embedded in the addiction can be the fantasy that the altered state will provide a spiritual connection which will protect the person from everyday life.
- Is their need to have this experience a hedonistic indulgence? If so, the experience is likely to be of minimal value. If it is authentic it needs to be integrated into consciousness and manifested positively in the external world (e.g., a focus on service to others).
- Does the experience of the altered state or engagement in the cycle of use divert or distract the person from addressing their psychological issues? This diversion or distraction may be conscious or unconscious, but the result is a potential emotional tsunami that grows the longer the issues are not attended to. It also creates a multitude of issues that are associated with the addiction itself.

Taking these points into account while keeping in mind the definitions of spirituality discussed earlier raises a key question: *Does substance and process use enhance the individual's sense of self in the world and make them more responsible or accountable to themselves and others?*

There needs to be growth in the person's psychological development, a broadening and 'owning' of who they are as an individual as well as their contribution to the collective community. Over time, an addiction has the opposite effect – it reduces a person's capacity to be present for themselves and those around them. When working with patients we need to find a language through which to understand their addiction. At one level, there is a common language and shared experience that comes with the cycle of addiction, which is why attending support groups and other treatment groups can be very important, particularly during the initial phases of abstinence. Identifying with others can be of benefit as the person may feel a sense of normalcy in what they are experiencing and, in some instances, they may need to look to others for hope and role models as to what lies ahead in their recovery.

At another level however, the person with an addiction also needs to understand that their relationship with their addiction is unexampled: ultimately, they need to move beyond the rhetorical language of the collective to find their own vocabulary and phraseology for their addiction. There can be the benefit of inclusivity with others that comes through sharing a common experience, but what is also required is an understanding of the uniqueness of the person's individual experience of their addiction.

There are some patients who cannot find a language for what they want to express; instead, their addiction *is* their attempt to communicate. This leads to the following reflection.

Why individuals are 'drawn' to certain addictions

Repetitive behaviours in the form of an addiction are often the patient's presenting issue and usually they see this cycle as the *source* of their distress rather than a *symptom*. They believe that if they could only stop the cycle, they would regain control over their life. Even if or when they attain abstinence, there is still a lack of awareness of what is driving their cycle. There are also patients who simply do not have the words to explain their persistent need to re-engage with their addiction. In these cases, therapists can help by starting to think about what the patient is projecting onto their addiction and what they are communicating through their behaviours.

This approach draws on Jung's understanding that "[t]he general psychological reason for projection is always an activated unconscious that seeks expression" (1977, para. 352). Therefore, the addiction is a manifestation of projections from an unconscious that is seeking expression. This view also rests on Jung's observation that the symptomatology of an illness is an attempt at some form of integration (1969, para. 312). In other words, *if we see addictive behaviour as symptoms of an illness, these symptoms are, if understood correctly, a natural attempt at healing some sort of sickness.*

Seen in this way, what a person projects onto their addiction is an aspect of themselves that has split off and seeks integration. Therapists need to understand this unconscious communication and be willing to be informed and learn from it. For example, the addiction and associated ritual cycle and attendant emotions can indicate what was potentially lost or lacking in their earliest relationships, including babyhood and in utero. The baby's experience of being in the womb and post-birth can be thought of as examples of 'participation mystique', which is a non-reflective state that cannot distinguish between fantasy and reality (Levy-Bruhl, cited in Stein 1995). Participation mystique is a pre-symbolic state that can border on hallucinatory, and Jung uses this term to describe a state of non-differentiation – in other words, an individual's original unconscious state, out of which consciousness can develop (Jung, cited in Samuels et al. 1991). For someone who metaphorically wants to be 'carried' and escape from the responsibilities and hardships of life, this undifferentiated state can be highly desirable to the extent that they continually attempt to re-experience it. This can be understood as a desire to re-experience the sensation of 'oceanic bliss': of being in the womb.

Returning to the idea of the patient using an addiction (through projection) to communicate the losses in their early relationship, it is worth considering they may not have language for their addiction because their experience of loss, lack, or trauma may be pre-verbal or pre-cognitive. The impact of the mother on the baby and the impression that is left is described by Elizabeth Noble:

> Imagine that you and I were to spend nine months together in a small enclosed space. At the end of this time you would have many opinions and assumptions about yourself and me. Likewise, each of us leaves the womb with profound impressions that influence the rest of our life.
>
> (1993, p. 25)

Karl Stern includes participation mystique in the image of maternal relationship as he writes that the:

> [w]oman in the person of our mother, is the first being with whom we are in contact ... It all begins with a true fusion of being ... the child is an extension of the mother without clearly perceptible borders. There exists a *participation mystique,* a psychic flow from mother to child and from child to mother.
>
> (Stern, cited in Bradshaw 1990, p. 81)

What is evident from these two quotes is that the baby is undoubtedly impacted by the mother's psychological and physical state. The mind, body and spirit of both mother and baby are influenced and imprinted from this connection which has permanent effects on the individual. A baby cannot intellectually know or fully describe what experiences were contaminating or harmful in utero or during baby-hood. However, the dynamics within the therapeutic relationship can provide some sense of the atmosphere within this early state of participation mystique.

The residue of these early experiences can be communicated by the patient's memories and their piecing together of the accounts of others' memories around their conception, their mother's pregnancy, and post-birth experience. These accounts are important, but so too are the patient's understanding of these events, especially how they have internalised these narratives in their fantasy of what occurred. The therapist sensitively uses this information to explore the patient's subjective interiority. Some patients want to focus solely on 'objective facts' as a way of defending against their potentially overwhelming emotional inner world. Patients can also want to find the 'factual truth' to justify their emotional reality because they do not trust that they themselves or others will understand or believe their emotional truth if it is not backed up by 'facts'.

There are circumstances when the factual truth (e.g., neglect, trauma or abuse) does need to be exposed and requires action, sometimes legal, to make others accountable. This process can enable the patient to move forward in their thera-peutic process, but it can also re-traumatise them. The therapist needs to hold in mind the details, and how the patient has internalised these details, as well as how they are living with the objective and subjective dimensions of their early history.

Sometimes details, or fragments of details, that cannot be cognitively recalled can begin to form within the merged zone of participation mystique. This can be evident in the therapeutic relational dynamics and through the presentation of images, dreams, reverie, synchronicities and symbolism. The 'feeling tones' and the shifts in these tones can be a useful gauge in the clinical setting, and these will be explored through my work with Chloe.

My initial countertransference reaction to Chloe was 'you are too much', and that I would never be able to give her enough of what she needed. During sessions I struggled to stay focused on what I experienced as her diatribe of details and associated melodramatics. I was aware that I looked forward to the end of the sessions. Chloe's desperate need for my undivided attention was so intense that I would sometimes be left emotionally fragmented. On occasions when her neediness became overwhelming, I would collapse afterwards into a floating half-slumber as if I had been anaesthetised. I would fight falling asleep during our sessions by blinking and clenching my muscles. This was also an attempt to wake my body up as it felt like a dead weight. There was no relational intimacy between us; I was simply observing Chloe and giving her what she needed to facilitate her immediate survival.

My emotional experience was an example of 'projective identification' (McWilliams 1994). This is an unconscious process whereby aspects of the patient's self or significant aspects of persons or relationships they have internalised are split off and attributed to a person, place or thing. These projected aspects may be felt by the projector to be either good or bad. Sometimes the therapist onto whom these projections fall experiences them as their own feelings or thoughts, as I did with Chloe. I was identifying with (and feeling as my own) her own unconscious conviction that she was 'too much' and that 'I would never be able to give her enough of what she needed'. This reflective work can be described as 'reverie'. James Grotstein offers an example of healthy reverie in which the mother catches her infant's torment and transforms it into meaning through thought and language (2000, p. 12).

After sitting with Chloe for numerous sessions during which time I was immersed in reverie, countertransference, projections and projective identifications, she shared her early history for the first time. Previously, she simply did not have wondering, interest or access to her early history or pre-symbolic layers of her experience. Through our work together and my holding of the therapeutic container, her history started to come together, and I could see and feel what had been shaping my experience of working with her. Metaphorically speaking, it was as if the pieces of a jigsaw puzzle had placed themselves together without any intervention from me. It was humbling and enlivening to have my unspoken and unshared reverie made sense of by Chloe telling her story. This is what happened when the countertransferential struggle I described earlier suddenly made sense, as Chloe spoke for the first time about her first year of life.

As time passed Chloe seemed increasingly exhausted with herself in sessions. Her reporting of the details of the weekend would fall flat and the themes became routinely predictable and blended into one another. As she stopped filling the space with a repetitive narrative there was room for new material to emerge and she started to draw together her history in a way she had not done previously. The feeling tone in the room changed: the frenzied energy became calm and considered. I listened intently to Chloe's memories and recollections and felt alive with interest and care. Chloe described herself as being an anticipated baby, wanted and planned by both parents. Her mother had low-level nausea for most of the day for the first 16 weeks of her pregnancy but apart from that, there was nothing noteworthy. The only exception was her mother's hormonally based migraines which were reduced to manageable headaches during the pregnancy. This was a welcome relief. However, post-birth, Chloe's mother's migraines returned and they were so severe that her mother had to take strong medication that made her sleep for hours on end. This resulted in Chloe being left in her cot, bouncer or play pen. Chloe could not be breastfed in case the medication was transferred in her mother's milk. Consequently, she was bottle-fed and her mother would set an alarm approximately every four hours to wake herself up so that she could feed her baby.

My fantasy was that when Chloe was being fed, changed and generally tended to, she received what she needed from her mother and this attention was not just a somatic relief but a euphoric 'hit'. However, once her mother's attention went elsewhere, for example, to rest, take medication or meet other domestic responsibilities, Chloe would be left longing. I hypothesise that she experienced a sense of bodily lost-ness and disorientation when her mother 'left'. This alternation between heightened attention when she was tended to by her mother followed by the drop into bottomless nothingness created a relational patterning for Chloe that expressed itself in her addictive cycle.

The defensive manifestation of this cycle was her desperate need to hold peoples' attention which she accomplished in several ways: by entertaining them and reading their moods; by monitoring her emotional barometer as she became what she thought they wanted her to be; and by buoying her friends up with the excitement of cocaine on weekends. She would swing from the anticipated 'high' of the night to being alone and repeatedly experiencing absence, scrolling through social media and seeing other parties that she had not been invited to, or the one she had organised having no photos of her posted.

Over the course of our work Chloe clearly saw how her need to control the attention she got from others pushed them away. She also recognised that she did not see her friends for who they were, only as people who could temporarily ease her loneliness. She knew she needed to stop the weekend cycle of cocaine use, which morphed into compulsive online dating if she did not use. Her fear of being alone felt insurmountable: without both behaviours she faced a vast loneliness.

It is impossible to know someone's in utero or early experiences. However, there is a possibility that their addiction and associated ritual is used to comfort themselves by re-experiencing the visceral familiarity of the mother/baby relationship. It can also be an attempt to *process* early relational rupture. There may be a fear of what will be discovered if the patient abstains and addresses their addiction. This can manifest as a powerful pull to relapse or divert their obsessive attention onto something or someone else.

The pull of the addiction

An addiction can appear to provide a predictable companionship without the difficulties and complexities of real relationships. Depending on its severity, an addiction can be extremely detrimental to someone's relationship with themselves and others. What can be confusing for the patient is that the behaviour that turns into an addiction can start out as a way of facilitating a relationship with oneself and with others. The patient may be able to acknowledge the destructiveness of their addiction, or they may be in denial. Either way, there is usually a loyalty to their addiction, even if they hate it at the same time. There are obvious reasons why people become addicted and stay addicted, and there are secondary reasons for practising an addiction which, themselves, can become addictive. These secondary addictions are not always immediately apparent and may not be revealed until the person ceases their use or engages in therapy.

The following are some examples of *why* people continue to practise an addiction, even when it is starting to damage them, their life, and the lives of others around them:

a *A constant companion.* A person whose childhood experiences were marked by inconsistency and untrustworthiness may be drawn to the consistency and emotional reliability offered by addiction and its associated ritual. When life does not go the way a person with a fragile inner world wants or needs it to, they may become emotionally, cognitively, existentially overwhelmed and their addiction acts as a trusted companion that not only comforts and soothes, but does not question, challenge or judge them.

b *A buffer for life.* When someone's life is structured around an addictive cycle, they are living their emotions, thoughts and behaviours *within* this cycle. The practice of addiction and its rituals buffer or fend off what needs to be addressed or responded to in life, ranging from unresolved grief to day-to-day responsibilities. In this way they end up living in the parallel universe of their addiction.

c *A way of coping.* The addiction may be a person's way of getting through the week, the day, or the hour as it falsely promises a release which serves as a motivational strategy. This self-management system can be *discovered*, or it can be *learned* from role models who lack ways of dealing with life without using some form of substance or process. For some patients, their life experience means that the idea of not using a mind-altering substance when coping with grief or celebration is a foreign concept.

d *The addiction holds history.* A person's addiction may have attended all their milestones, turning points, social events, holidays, places lived, and personal and professional relationships. It can function as a metaphorical photo album.

e *Addiction provides an identity.* The patient may feel that, as a person, they have nothing to offer and that there is nothing special or interesting about them. In this case, their addiction can provide an identity – it has a set of thoughts, feelings and behaviours they can live into which provides direction and purpose. This identity can also be shared with others, because in addiction there is common language, interest and shame. Certain addictions are necessary for membership into particular subcultures.

f *Life and spirituality on your terms.* The addicted patient wants to live and experience spirituality on their terms, not on life's terms. They are controlling their spirituality as their connection to 'something greater than themselves' is generated from their wants and expectations, not from what life presents or offers. These patients exist in the hope that by doing something over and over they will be satisfied and their inner void will be filled. They may insist to themselves and others that they are opening something up through their addiction, but the repetitious nature of addiction means they are in fact shutting down their creativity and spirituality.

g *Addiction covers pain.* An addiction can be used to cover primary pain that is too unbearable to be explored or expressed. It may be easier for the patient to talk about their addiction and the struggles surrounding its cycle than a deep-seated pain that they do not really know, or do not know how to express. For example, a patient may feel shame that they need to keep hidden at all costs, especially if they feel they are to blame for being the source of it. The addiction can be used as a safer outlet so that their underlying pain can be 'spoken about' through the addiction. The patient may not know they are using their addiction in this way because the emotions that have been suppressed mirror the emotions and torment that are enacted in the addictive cycle. Either way, these emotions are not being processed fully as they are being 'spoken' through a false channel. Lastly, for some patients it can be more acceptable to speak about their addiction as they experience it as a force outside their control and this absolves them of responsibility.

h *Staying connected to the family system.* Human beings have an inherent need to belong and be part of a family or collection of people, structures and community. When there is a lack of healthy emotional connectedness between members of such groups, the actual use of the substance or process, or the common need to alter one's state in order to manage life, can operate as a binding agent. Replicating the behaviours and values of parents, family members and close friends can also be a conscious or unconscious attempt to belong. Stepping outside of spoken and unspoken family rules can leave a person metaphorically homeless – ridiculed or shunned as a warning to others not to do the same. To be 'on the outer' in this way can be very lonely and this experience can be triggered when someone first starts treatment and questions or challenges their family system.

It can be extremely hard for an individual to live in *opposition* to the family message that has been subliminally ingrained throughout their upbringing.

Often the adult part of a patient says, "I do not want to treat my partner, my children (or myself) as I was treated, but I don't know any other way: I cannot stop it". Overtly, the adult self is desperate to live differently but this is in opposition to the assimilated, covert pull towards the family message which says,

> I must damage myself (and my children and partner) in the way I was damaged, so that we can connect to each other through the familial damage system which is what I know. That's what makes my family (and me) special – it is who we *are.*

Behaving in this way is a passport to acceptance in the family – it is saying, "I am just like you; please will you now accept and love me?" Another common feature is when the child of the addicted parent wants to be seen and loved for who they are, rather than through the eyes of the parent's addiction. This child's pleas are, "Aren't I enough for you? If you really loved me, you would give it up", and "Aren't I worth living for?"

i   *Addiction as a framework for madness.* An addiction can provide a framework to contain a personality disorder. The patient would rather have the consequences and emotions of the addiction than the maddening, overwhelming distress of the personality-disordered traits. They may fear that once they start spiralling into their crazed inner state they will never recover. They may feel that their addiction is all that stands between them and this fate, and I will explore further this association in the next point.

Relationship between an addiction and a personality disorder

A personality disorder is, at its core, disturbed and disturbing. This disturbance expresses itself as thoughts, feelings, and behaviours that are expressed intrapsychically and interpersonally, and manifest in various forms ranging from subtle manipulation to intractable rage. Depending on the actual disorder, a person can experience their self as a fluctuating field of emptiness, anger, desperation, agitation, resentment and loneliness. An addiction can be used to anaesthetise, contain or distract oneself from these intense states. It can also fraudulently fill an empty inner life by creating ritual to contain what the person does not want to experience; for example, the 'obligatory' glass of wine used to mark the end of the working day that inevitably turns into a whole bottle in order to blot out a sense of hopelessness and loneliness.

An individual with a personality disorder tries to control their world and the people in it and an addiction can provide solace and refuge from the utter frustration of not being in total control. This induced solace is inauthentic and can only soothe and serve the ego – its anaesthetic, mind-numbing quality means that it can never facilitate the development of psychological awareness. These patients can convince themselves that the solace they derive from their addiction is a mark of their specialness and is indicative of their capacity for 'illuminating' and 'creative' experiences. In reality, it is a contrived substance- or process-induced state, driven by a need to escape from their inability to relinquish their fantasy of control and accept life on life's terms.

When an addiction masks a personality disorder, the severity of this pathology may not be obvious until the patient actively abstains, decides to abstain, or at least attempts to abstain. This threat of abstinence challenges the scaffolding that props up their troubled self and the therapist can begin to see glimpses of the disordered self within. At this point the therapist needs to assess the patient's capacity to engage in symbolic thought and make use of their capacity for imagining. When referring to a patient's capacity to symbolise, I am talking about their ability to hold what is known consciously by their ego while also being open and curious about the emerging unknown, the unconscious. Key to this capacity is being able to distinguish between personal fantasy and reality and acknowledge that reality may not be what they want it to be. A symbolic function is not something you do or do not have – it is a changing spectrum of positions ranging from the negation of reality to the ability to entertain that reality contains absence and lack (Colman 2006).

Having a symbolic function enables us to communicate, to put emotions into words, and to be able to take the raw material of sensation, images and stories and give language to them. When this involves another person there is an interplay of communicative digestion and processing and understanding of one's own mind while being open and curious to another. Specifically, the therapist needs to determine whether the patient can:

- imagine what life would be like without their addiction, and be able to wonder who they would become; or
- answer questions; or, when questioned, do they defensively hold onto their addiction and justify their use, refusing blatantly to entertain a life without it.

The former position highlights the capacity for flexible symbolic thought and an ability to imagine life without the addiction as well as the likely consequences of not using. The latter position has no space for change, for imagining the ongoing consequences of the addiction, or to have anything come between the individual and their addiction. This life is entirely structured around the demands of the addiction and there is no room to challenge or confront it. Giles Clark provides a perspective on this when he writes:

> Addictive- and personality-disordered states tend to be so un-empathic and emotionally manipulative that there can be no symbolic linking, no real imaginal life, no honest critical reflection, no recognition of the subjectivity of projections, no relational alterity and no symbolisation.

(2014, p. 147)

In light of this, the need to assess the patient's capacity to symbolise is paramount – it is the deciding factor in the direction of their treatment, both in individual therapy and in terms of enlisting other treatment options. If the patient is assessed incorrectly, they may be 'set up to fail', which will only lead to an increased need to return to their addiction, further entrenching their personality-disordered traits. On a more optimistic note, Clark points out that if the patient does engage in the therapeutic process, there is the potential that "this fundamental wound and all-permeating hurt are reached and its abject grief or utter despair is expressed, mourning that engenders real symbolisation may emerge" (2014, p. 147).

Through the therapeutic process, there is hope that the patient will develop a capacity to symbolise, even if it is very minimal. An inherent quality in symbolic thinking is empathy (Clark 2014). Empathy can be a motivating factor in a person's decision to attempt to abstain and change their behaviour, as they see the damage they are doing to those around them, and they can be emotionally impacted by this. In my experience, patients rarely want to let the substance or process go – it is the consequences of the addiction they cannot live with anymore and this can force them to unwillingly address their addictive use. These consequences typically include physical or mental health issues, financial hardships, destructive relationships or institutional intervention. To support this work, therapy needs to address the patient's pathology and unintegrated losses and traumas. This strengthens their ego and potentially clears the way for a healthy individuation process to occur.

Spiritus contra spiritum

The translation of the Latin phrase, *spiritus contra spiritum*, is 'spirit against spirit'. This phrase was used by Jung in response to a letter from Bill Wilson, co-founder of Alcoholics Anonymous (A.A.). In this letter, Wilson sought Jung's opinion about his treatment of a former patient who had consulted Jung about his alcoholism. It was Jung's belief that a spiritual intervention is required as a remedy for the spirit when working with an alcoholic. His observation can be understood as: if the patient is to recover, they need a spiritual experience instead of looking for a metaphorical spirit in a bottle. The hypothesis is that the patient needs to seek higher forms of spiritual experience to counter the depraving effects of lower forms of spirit. In this section, I propose that this relates to patients with addictions in general, not only alcoholism.

In his response to Wilson, Jung specifies some defining features of a spiritual experience, and how a person can open themself up to such an experience:

> The only right and legitimate way to such an experience is that it happens to you in reality, and it can only happen to you when you walk on a path which leads you to higher understanding. You might be led to that goal by an act of grace or through a personal and honest contact with friends, or through a higher education of the mind beyond the confines of mere rationalism.

(1976, p. 625)

Jung's comments on the nature of spiritual experiences will be separated into five points and expanded upon with clinical importance and application:

- '... happens to you in reality'. The necessary spiritual experience must occur when the individual has a sufficient grasp on 'reality', that is, the ego is strong enough to be able to process cognitively what has occurred.
- '... walk on a path which leads you to higher understanding'. The 'path' refers to an individual's inherent human drive towards self-development and that this experience must be integrated in a way that expands self-awareness. This 'higher understanding' entails a commitment to ongoing psychological growth.
- '... led to that goal by an act of grace'. I suggest that in this comment Jung is pointing to our dependency on a power greater than ourselves. This can be conceptualised in many ways from a personal God through to the *telos* of the psyche which is wholeness. The form grace takes is irrelevant; what is important is that the recipient receives it in a way that deeply touches their humanity, and they experience the essence of unconditional love. This gift then needs to be integrated into what Jung calls a higher understanding.
- '... through a personal and honest contact with friends'. These words refer to the development of a life based on connections with friends, partners, children, family members or a community that is deeply impactful, continuing to touch the individual in an unforgettable way. Repeated encounters with honest reflections from a person we respect can motivate us to want to take responsibility and better ourselves. This honesty between people can occur when someone enters a meaningful relationship, becomes a parent, experiences illness or the death of a loved one.
- '... or through a higher education of the mind beyond the confines of mere rationalism'. This final point refers to psychological, spiritual or philosophical learning that cannot be processed or understood logically. Encounters with these dimensions of experience present the individual with an opportunity to keep an open mind about the nature of learning and wisdom, and understand that not everything of importance can be explained by reason.

In the following section I will use the terms spiritual experience and spiritual intervention interchangeably. It is *the patient* who determines whether or not they have had a spiritual intervention, not the therapist, nor anyone else. Such experiences are subjective, and their importance can only be measured by the individual. Nonetheless, clinicians need to assess the strength of the patient's ego and their capacity for symbolic thought as this indicates whether they may be susceptible to delusional or psychotic states. The therapist must be able to discern if their patient is internalising and distorting a spiritual experience in such a way that supports or reinforces their disturbed self or addiction.

If the patient has sufficient ego strength and capacity to symbolise, the therapist can be open to their narrative and not critique whether their experience is spiritual or not, even though it may be outside the realm of the therapist's comprehension.

For some patients, this experience is deeply personal, and they may not want to share it for fear that doing so will diminish its profundity. They may also fear the therapist will exploit or distort their experience through interpretation. However, it is beneficial to explore how the patient holds onto that which is deeply personal to them within the therapeutic relationship, because this may parallel their capacity to hold onto what is of great value to them in day-to-day life. It does not matter whether a patient shares their spiritual experience with their therapist; what matters is the impact of this experience and the way they integrate it into their life.

A spiritual intervention can leave a person overwhelmed and bewildered or can be a very subtle illumination. Regardless of the form it takes, the experience is profound and becomes a defining moment in a person's life. They are usually faced with a 'choice'. They either cease the addictive behaviour and work through the grief and consequences, opening up the possibility of a different way of living, or continue the cycle which will ultimately lead to the destruction of themselves and others. They are confronted with the reality that a life lived solely within a rational and materialistic frame is one-dimensional. These values are not necessarily incompatible with spirituality. However, if an addicted person is to recover, they must accept that life has other dimensions in which they need to live if they are to become well and remain well. In order to do this, they must let go of their ego-based expectations about how life should treat them and who they think they are or should be. Instead, life must be lived as a journey to an unknown destination.

A spiritual experience can be a pivotal point for the direction of one's life and can also be a catalyst for individuation. Furthermore, if individuation is to be ongoing the person must find their way into a 'spiritual life'. This way of living encompasses an understanding that the unconscious is larger than the conscious self, and that their unconscious is dynamic and has a creativity to it as well as a destructiveness. Such spiritual experiences may occur within the life-long individuation process and provide a sense of comfort that one is on the 'right path', as well as providing guidance and caution.

In contrast, trying to resist the selfishness of the addiction on willpower alone is tormenting and crazy-making because the addiction is entirely focused on the pursuit of a hedonistic experience which involves the user and nobody else, unless the other can be used as a prop or enabler. The addicted person's fantasy that they can beat or break their addiction without any external support must fail – the addiction is like a virus that keeps mutating to stay alive and is more resourceful than the ego's efforts to stop it.

Consequently, if the addicted person does not commit to engaging in life in a different way, they are at the mercy of their addiction whose insidious control will destroy their physical and mental health, as well as their relationship with themselves and others. To reiterate, I am talking about addictions in general, which includes substances, processes, and relationships, as well as internet use, work, and the pursuit of an ideal body image. If a person with an addiction *does* commit to the courageous challenge of ceasing their addiction, they have to understand they cannot do this alone and that sustaining abstinence requires ongoing maintenance of the following:

Discipline. This comprises a semi-formal or formal structure that provides a holding container. The addicted person needs to participate in this container physically and psychologically and has a responsibility to attend regularly. Examples include individual or group therapy, a recovery programme, meditation or a spiritual community.

Service. The individual must live their life based on being 'of service' to others and learn that only by giving do we receive.

Gratitude. This relates to the development of an inherent appreciation and thankfulness for one's good fortune and that of others.

It is worth noting that all these qualities have an external focus. The intention of having an awareness of others and a responsibility to them can act as a motivator, prompting them to look outside of themselves, instead of retreating within and acquiescing to the enduring, cunning and seductive call of the addiction.

When a patient makes the decision to seriously address their addiction and live from a different narrative, their needs must be assessed to ascertain whether they require specialist treatment such as detoxification, in-patient or out-patient rehabilitation, structured engagement in a formal recovery programme, or participation in a recovery-facilitating project. If the patient does not want to engage with these supports, the therapist must think honestly and carefully about whether they can provide the necessary treatment for their patient's new way of living; if they cannot, they may be setting the patient up to fail. Sometimes increasing the number of weekly sessions will suffice, and sometimes the patient will use this as an 'easy option' because it is not as threatening as engaging with other services.

When a patient comes to a crossroads and the decision must be made that can change the trajectory of their life, the therapist must be able to acknowledge the highly sensitive nature of the patient's predicament, and the insidious all-encompassing nature of their addiction. At this point the patient may question the therapist's personal experience of an addiction.

Can you work with addicts if you have never been an addict yourself?

This question has been omnipresent in the contexts in which I have worked. When I worked in the 'Alcohol and Other Drug Department' in an institutional setting, patients asked me outright about my 'addict status'. I assume that their aim was to determine whether I belonged to 'us' or 'them'. If I belonged to 'us', meaning I was an ex-addict, I was clean and sober and my intent was to 'convert' them to whatever recovery system I had used successfully. If I was one of 'them', meaning I had never been an addict, I was a naive academic with probable voyeuristic tendencies and therefore easy to manipulate. (There are certain contexts, particularly in group settings whereby disclosing one's 'addiction' status and the way in which this is used for the treatment of the patient is beneficial. However, I will not be discussing these contexts in any detail here.)

In private practice this question was rarely asked, presumably due to the frame and setting in which I work. Nonetheless, I am certain my patients would wonder whether I had experienced addiction and what my stance is in relation to the use of certain substances and processes. This curiosity about the therapist is normal and healthy as it reflects the patient's ability to be aware of the other; the patient who shows no interest in the therapist or their reactions may be of more concern as this can indicate an underlying pathology. Regardless of the context, when a therapist is working with patients who are addicted, the therapist needs to carefully consider the following points:

- The patient needs to stay in *their* process and have *their own* experience of recovery. If the therapist has a history of addiction and 'shares' their process of recovery the patient can try to mimic that process. The patient is in a vulnerable state, wanting direction and approval, and they can forfeit their own process and instead follow the guidance and prescribed steps of their therapist. The patient may think 'if it worked for my therapist and they seem well adjusted, their path will work for me'. Of course, no-one can use someone else's path in this way – the patient who tries to copy the therapist does not experience the necessary 'lost-ness' which is essential for authentic individuation. Also, if the patient's experience is different to their therapist's they may feel inadequate and like a failure as they know their therapist overcame their addiction while they are still struggling.
- The therapist must reflect on their process in terms of individual and familial history of addictions, compulsions and obsessions, in both their personal therapy and supervision. If they do not have adequate self-awareness and clarity about what their process is and what it is not, they may see their patient's abstinence as their own success, and any relapse as their own failure. They may disproportionality identify and invest in their patient that places an inordinate, unconscious pressure on the patient and can lead them to re-engage in their addictive behaviour. It can be confusing for the patient to know how to respond to this unspoken *investment* that originates from their therapist.
- The question of whether addiction is genetic or not inevitably arises, particularly when there is an intergenerational history of such behaviours. When working with a patient, it is crucial to explore why they believe it is 'nature', 'nurture', or 'a mixture of the two', as this exploration can provide valuable information that leads to greater awareness of their addiction and potential recovery. As therapists, it is impossible not to have wonderings about this question, and certainly we all have leanings towards a particular position, but it is important the therapist suspends their beliefs in the service of their patient's exploration.
- The question of whether the therapist has had their own addiction can come from the patient's desperate longing for hope. The patient may have

repeatedly tried and failed to turn their life around, unable to compete with the power of their addiction. They want someone to hold 'hope' for them when they do not have hope themselves. Crucially, however, this hope needs to be conveyed through the *disposition* of the therapist *not* through motivational enthusiasm or self-disclosure. The disposition of the therapist emerges from their own process of individuation, in which a history of addiction may or may not feature.

- The patient's questioning of the therapist's addiction status can also come from their need to determine whether the therapist 'knows' the destructiveness that comes with this cycle. The patient is anticipating and evaluating whether the therapist has the capacity to be able to tolerate, sustain and survive the darkness of this exploration.

- Nonetheless, as much as the therapist may want to hold the frame, patients with an addiction history are particularly adept at accessing such information even if they know the other does not want to give it. The therapist may feel cornered or seduced which can result in an 'enactment'. This unintended disclosure can leave the therapist bewildered at how they have come to behave in a way which is totally at odds with their professional principles. What matters, when such a transgression occurs, is that the therapist uses it to develop more awareness of the insidious and manipulative nature of addiction, and that experienced therapists can still be hoodwinked.

- My own sense is that, in a room of several hundred people, a person with a history of addiction will find others with the same history very quickly because of their capacity to detect people with a similar wound. Such patients are looking for the same wound in the therapist, although they *will* work with the therapist whose process of individuation has taken them to the depths of their own wounds, regardless of whether addiction is part of that story. Even so, in the clinical context it can feel as if the patient has an almost 'telepathic' sense around whether the therapist has personally experienced addiction and, again, this can be very disconcerting. When this occurs, the therapist must hold onto their authenticity and feel confident in their clinical competence by holding the therapeutic frame in a non-defensive way.

Conclusion

When working with this kind of patient there can be an ever-present threat of destruction. In cases where this threat becomes a reality, it can lead to an annihilation of relationships or physical and mental health, and possible consequences include death, violence and institutionalisation. In the face of this, the 'service' the therapist provides is to 'bear witness'. Halifax describes this as:

> ... the practice of being fully present and connected with our whole being to the full catastrophe, neutrality, or joy of whatever is arising. Even more deeply, the practice of Bearing Witness is about being in an unfiltered relationship with

others and the world around us, as well as ourselves, and coming alongside with open hands and open heart.

(2012, p. 40)

The environment offered by the therapist needs to comprise a capacity to bear witness plus clinical expertise and theoretical knowledge. This includes personal therapy and supervision, and provision of a therapeutic container that is congruent with who they are as a person and practitioner. When the therapist has these in place they are in a better position to cope if the patient is irreparably damaged by their addiction, although it can still be extremely difficult for the therapist to integrate and live with such outcomes.

Finally, the therapist must understand that destruction and creation are inseparable; a person cannot have one without the other and both are necessary for psychological growth. An addiction can simply destroy and there is no psychological awareness gained, or it can be a turning point for a person to create a new way of life and set forth on the path of individuation. A spiritual experience may be a catalyst, or it may occur on that path – either way it is the psyche's way of intervening to destroy a redundant way of living and offer another path that enhances the individual's being in the world.

References

Bradshaw, J. (1990). *Homecoming.* New York: Bantam Books.

Clark, G. (2014). 'Symbolising and not-symbolising' in Pickering, J. & Samuel, G. (eds.) *Collected writings of Giles Clark: Recycling madness with Jung, Spinoza and Santayana.* London: Routledge, pp. 135–160.

Colman, W. (2006). 'Imagination and the imaginary', *Journal of Analytical Psychology,* 51(1), pp. 21–41.

Freud, S. (1917). 'Mourning and melancholia' in Strachey, J. (ed.) *The standard edition of the complete psychological works of Sigmund Freud.* Vol. 14. London: Hogarth Press, pp. 237–258.

Groff, C. & Groff, S. (1990). *The stormy search for the self: A guide to personal growth through transformational crisis.* New York: Penguin Putnam Inc.

Grotstein, J. S. (2000). *Who is the dreamer who dreams the dream?* New York: Routledge .

Halifax, J. (2018). *Standing at the edge: Finding freedom where fear and courage meet.* New York: Flatiron Books.

Jung, C. G. (1958). *The collected works of C. G. Jung. Volume 11: Psychology and religion: West and East.* Edited by Read, H., Fordham, M., & Adler, G. Translated by Hull, R. F. C. Princeton, NJ: Princeton University Press.

Jung, C. G. (1969). *The collected works of C. G. Jung. Volume 8: The structure and dynamics of the psyche.* 2nd edn. Edited by Read, H., Fordham, M., & Adler, G. Translated by Hull, R. F. C. Princeton, NJ: Princeton University Press.

Jung, C. G. (1971). *The collected works of C. G. Jung. Volume 6: Psychological types.* 2nd edn. Edited by Read, H., Fordham, M., & Adler, G. Translated by Hull, R. F. C. Princeton, NJ: Princeton University Press.

Jung, C. G. (1976). *C. G. Jung. Letters, volume 2: 1951–1961.* Edited by Adler, G. Princeton, NJ: Princeton University Press.

Jung, C. G. (1977). *The collected works of C. G. Jung. Volume 18: The symbolic life.* 2nd edn. Edited by Read, H., Fordham, M., & Adler, G. Translated by Hull, R. F. C. Princeton, NJ: Princeton University Press.

McWilliams, N. (1994). *Psychoanalytic diagnosis: Understanding personality structure in the clinical process.* New York: The Guilford Press.

Noble, E. (1993). *Primal connections: How our experiences from conception to birth influence our emotions, behaviour, and health.* New York: Simon & Schuster.

Samuels, A., Shorter, B., & Plaut, F. (1991). *A critical dictionary of Jungian analysis.* London: Routledge.

Stein, M. (1995). *Encountering Jung: Jung on evil.* Princetown, NJ: Princeton University Press.

Stein, M. (2019). *Volume 1 of the collected writings of Murray Stein: Individuation.* Asheville, NC: Chiron.

Chapter 5

Psychopathic presentations

Can internal and external destruction and annihilation be associated with individuation?

Introduction

The introduction to this book provided an account of my early career work with a patient who killed himself while in a maximum-security institution. I explained how I wrestled for many years to explain his suicide and the impact working with him had on me. Twenty-five years have passed, and I will revisit this work and explore my post-treatment deliberations with hopefully more professional and personal maturity. I will also introduce this work conversation with another, more recent, presentation of psychopathy that occurred in my private practice. The final case studies that I discuss will be of private practice patients whose lives have been impacted by individuals with psychopathic tendencies.

The fundamental investigation of this chapter is: can a psychopath individuate? This question has been discussed in various psychological and sociological disciplines over many decades with psychopathy considered one of the most unchangeable and untreatable pathologies. The psychopath is understood as a person with substantially limited or entirely absent emotional capacity; guilt, remorse and empathy are not apparent. My own experience leads me to believe that there are at least two different presentations of psychopathy and the implications of these need to be understood before tackling the question of whether a psychopath can individuate. As we shall see, these two presentations of psychopathy have one aspect in common, which is a potentially disastrous and deadly impact on the people who encounter them, and on society at large.

The psychopath's effect on society presents itself in the news and is fodder for endless gruesome, crime-based stories and media coverage that captures people's attention. It is imperative to reflect on one's own intrigue with the people who dwell in these underworlds, and our motivations for engaging with the fictional and non-fictional representations of this human darkness. Such voyeurism does not prepare or anaesthetise someone who is truly infected by psychopathy. What gets into the system of the one contaminated is indelible and can force them into their own process of individuation.

In keeping with the approach taken in the previous chapters I will continue to explore patterns and insights which emerge from close examination and reflection

DOI: 10.4324/9781003558125-6

of my clinical experiences. The theories I refer to have been chosen because of their relevance to the cases presented, not as a literature review of psychopathy. I will also discuss some issues and disturbances that may arise for the therapist when working with this kind of patient and, again, my aim is not to provide definitive answers, but rather to activate curiosity, ideas and questions.

Part 1

This part begins with two in-depth case examples that will orientate the reader to different presentations of psychopathy. One in the context of a maximum-security institutional setting, and the other in private practice. Following this, the terms 'characterological psychopathy' and 'psychopathic pocket' will be defined and explained with the use of theories and academic references that are specifically chosen to meet the case examples. The therapist's countertransference responses, treatment considerations and hypotheses arising from these will also be discussed.

Part 2

The second part of this chapter comprises a discussion of the intersections, differences and similarities between 'maturation' and 'individuation'. The clinical questions that arise from this exploration are: 'Can maturation occur in a person with a psychopathic presentation?' and the principal question of this chapter: 'Can a psychopath individuate?' Both questions are reflected on through the lens of the case examples and a perspective is developed on whether, because of therapeutic treatment, the murderous darkness of psychopathy can become the basis of the development of some kind of self-responsibility.

Part 3

The final part discusses psychopathy and women. The combining of this pathology with women is atypical and unnerving. This section will cover an aspect of this seemingly unnatural association: the impact of psychopathic traits and how their enactment can result in life-long damage. Lastly, the therapist's responsibility when working with these patients is addressed.

The theme of psychopathy and individuation throughout this chapter is considered with specific Jungian, post-Jungian and psychoanalytic theories.

Part 1 – Case examples of psychopathic presentations

The following two case examples are men. The reason for this is that my experience in institutional settings was predominantly with men, and, in private practice, it has mostly been men who have expressed a high degree of violent and murderous fantasies towards others.

Case example 1 – Jimmy. Overview of history and presenting issues

Jimmy sought therapy out of boredom – it offered a break in the monotony of the maximum-security correctional institution in which he resided. As he was an informant he was housed in the classified witness protection prison for his own safety. He had been sentenced to 19 years in prison with a non-parole period of 15 years for murder. However, if Jimmy were able to provide credible evidence of alleged police corruption, his sentence would be reduced, and upon release he would be geographically relocated to an area that would ensure his anonymity. His daily routine rarely changed, and he had minimal, if any, control over how he spent his waking hours. The experience of being summoned from his cell and escorted to an interview room provided some variation to his predictable day – he could anticipate both his request being met and who would be escorting him. Being accompanied to or from the interview room gave him the opportunity to observe staff and other details within the environment, which he could potentially exploit in the future.

Jimmy had been known to the police for over 30 years. His first encounter was when he was four-years-old, and two police officers came to his family home after a call from the neighbours who had heard vulgar yelling and screaming. Subsequently, Jimmy's father was removed and taken to the station that night and charged with assault, intoxicated and disorderly conduct, and resisting arrest. Childhood abuse defined Jimmy's early years and I have no doubt his carefree attitude to killing resulted from his father's 'floggings' that would leave him unable to sit down for days. Jimmy had no respect for authority. He had witnessed and was the recipient of sadistic parenting which led him to internalise an offensive and immoral view of adults in charge. His mother increasingly numbed herself with alcohol and had no capacity to protect herself or her children from their father's abuse.

It is every prisoner's human right to have access to non-uniformed support services, and Jimmy took advantage of this privilege and sought therapy out of boredom. When I worked with Jimmy it felt like *he* was defining my role, not me, and he covertly coerced and directed me. As I was doing my job, I felt controlled and that I had lost my agency. I listened attentively to his stories which all concluded with him coming out on top at the expense of another. I learnt quickly that when my interventions did not fit his agenda, I would receive a penetrating, steely stare which served to remind me that he had the capacity to kill.

However, as our work continued, I started to wonder if there was another reason Jimmy had instigated therapy, and it was my countertransferential response of disgust, fear and despair that alerted me to the nature of this secondary gain. The sessions were his domain to indulge in his psychopathic recollections and re-visit the murder that he was charged with. As he did so, he took the 'life out of me' in the sessions, and I began to realise that 'taking life' was essential to Jimmy's psychological organisation.

His psychopathic disposition was obvious from an early age. He had to torment, and this need required an outlet. He told me about a class project in his very first year at school. The students were allocated a family of ducklings to look after under the guidance of the teacher. One morning, Jimmy went to school early and bludgeoned the ducklings with a hammer. He then positioned himself so he could watch his classmates eagerly race in to see the tiny ducks. Jimmy boastingly recalled that his favourite part was watching the children's excitement turn to distress as they saw the bloodied yellow feathers. Jimmy was the obvious offender as he was the only student who was not upset. When his father found out, he received similar treatment to the ducklings.

I slowly realised that the countertransference reactions stirred up by my work with Jimmy were divisive. I would either be overcome with sadness from listening to his history, or, righteously advocating for him to be punished. My position was one of rescuer or punisher and the latter would escalate when Jimmy tried to justify his crime. He believed with unwavering conviction that the murder he committed was an act of justice. He basked in a crusader's glow, claiming that he had saved the life of a defenceless child by killing her abusive mother. He had also victoriously exposed a corrupt police officer, and that would consequently save the lives of people within the community. His importance was reinforced by being a 'protected' prisoner who held classified information that had legal implications. Jimmy expressed no regret for his actions.

The sessions appeared to only reinforce his justifications and provide an opportunity for him to indulge his psychopathy. I was left questioning whether our work offered any benefit, specifically in terms of Jimmy's capacity to develop psychological responsibility. However, I thought I saw a glimmer of possibility that I had some therapeutic leverage when he said at the end of a session, "I like how you play strictly by the rules". I took these words as demonstrating that Jimmy had seen a quality in me. What was unclear and unimaginable at that time was how he would use this insight.

Case example 2 – Phillip. Overview of history and presenting issues

Phillip sought therapy out of necessity. He was fearful that his 'darkness' would destroy his marriage of six months. He was worried he would be left alone without the financial security and comfort of his third wife. Phillip did not want another failed relationship, and the thought of being single in his mid-60s frightened him. He was acutely aware that the pool of potentially available women had dwindled due to his diminished looks and sexual prowess; the physical and hormonal security that youth offered was no longer his. Also, he had retired from the armed forces which removed the opportunity to attend social events which opened the door to meeting women. To compensate for the end of his high-status career, Phillip needed the assurance of his marriage, which was potentially under threat because of what he described as his 'darkness'. This 'darkness' was not to be questioned or explored, but instead was a cryptic mystery that I had to actively silo. He firmly stipulated the two problematic areas he wanted to resolve in therapy.

The first area was his decline in social skills. When he was employed, Phillip had an endless supply of stories that he would inflate and embellish to engage his wife or whoever was his audience. Neighbours would say, "We would rather watch Phillip than the TV". However, he no longer had any material to source from his work, and no hobbies or activities to fall back on. Phillip had nothing to say, and his lack of available material threatened to expose his charismatic pretence that shielded a lost, insecure, damaged man. In an attempt to regain some sense of control and status, Phillip obsessively and compulsively searched the internet for footage of drone recordings from battlefronts. He would spend hours perusing footage of maimed soldiers crawling along the ground until they bled out and collapsed, and he would fixate on the faces of men seconds before they were mercilessly shot dead. This watching and witnessing became addictive, and was the second area he wanted to resolve through therapy.

Phillip's way of communicating had a transactional quality with occasional affective tones. He had a military bearing and was rigidly respectful. He treated me as a professional authority and had the expectation that I would take away the social awkwardness that arose when he had nothing to say or no stories to perform. Furthermore, he expected the therapy to alleviate or minimise his uncontrollable desire to venture into war footage. In the second session there was an obvious disparity of how we viewed the problems and how they would be addressed. I saw a lack of relational skills that required attention and exploration, whereas Phillip wanted to fill the lack with a polished veneer. Consequently, Phillip wanted to end the therapy, but his emerging depression gave him no option but to continue.

His depression had the same debilitating heaviness that he had first experienced as a young boy but had always managed to overcome with thrill-seeking behaviours such as street fighting and cruelty towards animals. He once strung up a dog on the branch of a tree to taunt his brother but loosened the rope when his sibling threatened to 'tell Mum'. It was not his mother's violence he feared; it was his mother instructing his father to 'pull him into line' that eventuated with Phillip being beaten by his father. Even though Phillip's father was violent, Phillip viewed him as weak and hated how he took orders from his wife without questioning or understanding what had occurred.

Thankfully Phillip channelled his contempt towards his parents into rugby. Playing the game was strangely comforting – there were set rules that a referee enforced and if a serious violation occurred, there would be a justifiable consequence. The physically demanding nature of the game and the structurally enforced rules provided Phillip with a calming reassurance when he was on the field. In addition, his early success in rugby meant that his mother was regarded positively in the community. This regard loosened her demands on her husband to discipline their son as she did not want his sporting performance affected. Phillip's mother lived through his achievements and rejoiced that he was revered for his 'killer instinct'.

When Phillip was 17, he fell in love with one of his teammate's sisters and although this was accompanied by honeymoon euphoria, there was also an emerging sadness that slowly developed into a depressive episode. His romance triggered memories of the loss of his mother who left his father four years earlier when Phillip was 13. His mother had become pregnant to Phillip's rugby coach and left Phillip and his family to begin her new life with her 'real' man, a man who would not take orders from her. Phillip's sadness and anger at his mother's abandonment were tightly encapsulated and suppressed. He superficially overcame his depression by joining the army and directed his unprocessed distress into regimented physical and psychological discipline which provided consistent validation for his respect of authority and politeness. Phillip embodied unwavering commitment to the armed forces. He subsequently married his first love who appreciated his impeccable manners, upstanding values and athletic appearance. They had four children in quick succession and were a tight insular unit as they all relocated with their father to his various postings. The children grew closer to their mother as she was the constant in their lives due to their father often being away. When Phillip was with them, he struggled to feel at ease in domestic life. He would rather be at work where he felt more relaxed as he knew what was expected of him.

After 46 years in the army Phillip retired. He was uncomfortable at home with his wife – they had little in common and when his children came to visit, he felt like an alien. Consequently, he had an affair to relieve his emotional disorientation, but this further isolated him from his family unit. To legitimise the affair as a 'real connection', he married the woman but their marriage dissolved within months as Phillip found her controlling and critical. This marital venture was an unconscious attempt to draw a veil over the loss of his first wife and the army, and it was not long before Phillip met someone else. However, this time he felt something that he had not previously felt in his relationships with women: fondness. This feeling towards another was intriguing, comforting and confusing for him, and was reason enough for him to agree to get married for the third time. As mentioned earlier, our work commenced six months into Phillip's third marriage. We established a rapport after numerous sessions working within the parameters of his agenda. Phillip accepted that his relational skills and addictive viewing were symptoms of his unprocessed history, and he knew he needed to continue his therapy and understand his relationship to his low-level depression.

I had mistakenly assumed that 'darkness' was his term for his depression, but what emerged was quite different. The darkness was a mental spasm that occurred in moments when he experienced a feeling akin to love. An example of this occurred when Phillip and his wife went away for a weekend at a peninsula renowned for its beauty. Phillip explained how, as they walked along a short bush track to enjoy the view, he felt unusually content, appreciating the ease and joviality of their banter. As they reached the viewing point, he noticed his wife looking at him with adoration and he was immediately overcome with disgust, and the thought that he wanted to 'wipe that pathetic look off her face'. As he felt this, he imagined pushing her over the barricade and off the cliff. He wrestled with this nearly overwhelming impulse. His wife noticed a sudden change in his eyes and was confused when he said he needed to step away as he had a fear of heights. Phillip was horrified and confused.

When he recounted this story, I could not understand or explain my countertransference reaction; however, the words that echoed in my mind were 'duplicitous' and 'fraudulent'. His own darkness seemed terrifying to him, and I took his sheepishness towards me as a fear that I would never want to see him again. Yet, at the same time, when he spoke of his impulsive cruelty, his posture was condescending and conceited, he had emotionally removed himself from the interaction, and was smugly observing my reaction. I was unnerved.

In the next section, I will introduce the term psychopathic pocket to reference the sudden need to annihilate that temporarily engulfed Phillip and differentiate it from Jimmy's characterological psychopathy in which annihilation is intrinsic and pervasive.

What is the distinction between someone who is characterologically psychopathic and someone who has a psychopathic pocket?

Definition of psychopathy

A psychopath belongs to a specific personality cluster of people who have a shameless disregard for others. They will violate or kill whatever or whoever is in the way of attaining their goals, without a trace of empathy. The original term 'psychopath' has since been replaced with 'antisocial personality disorder'. This current diagnostic description places importance on the violation of social and cultural norms; however, my focus is on interiority and psyche, and this is reflected in my use of the original term psychopath. This is also traditionally used in psychoanalytic literature.

Psychopath and psychopathy have their origin in the Greek language – 'psyche' relates to the soul and 'pathos' to suffering (Guggenbuhl-Craig 1980, p. 29). Therefore, a psychopath is a soul in suffering and psychopathy describes the collective characteristics of suffering souls. Seen in this way there is an overlap between psychopathy and individuation because the process of self-realisation requires the confrontation and integration of elements of one's psyche and the experience of pathos is an inevitable element of this process.

The other commonly used descriptions of psychopaths are that they are 'mentally ill' or 'psychologically sick'. Interestingly, it is people in the community that suffer from the psychopath's 'sickness', not the actual psychopath themselves. The psychopath may know at some level that they function differently but have no desire to overcome their suffering because they do not experience it as sickness. In treatment, the therapist is required to hold this incongruence along with the knowledge that the anti-social behaviour that results from the psychopath's sickness inflicts soul suffering on members of the community. This incompatibility in therapeutic agendas needs to be held in mind when working with these patients.

In my experience the central characteristic of the psychopath is their need to annihilate someone else's soul – they extinguish their victim's life force and want them to suffer. They do this because their own soul is innately suffering. They need to do to another person their version of what was done to them, or what is simply inherent in them. My definition of a psychopath is:

> someone who must put life to an end with callous and calculated intent. They need to annihilate something living and revel repeatedly in what they experience as their triumph. They take a conceited satisfaction from having remorselessly destroyed and having not been caught. This unshifting, relentless focal reality of psychopathy is so unnerving that it invites denial on behalf of the therapist. Nonetheless the cold, hard truth of the psychopathic patient needs to be acknowledged by the therapist, regarding who they are and the therapeutic role.

When working with psychopathy, diagnostic and theoretical language can be used as a splitting defence by the therapist, or it can anchor them to realistic expectations of treatment outcomes by puncturing their fantasies of how the patient will respond to therapy. Thus, it is crucial to determine what manifestation of psychopathy is being treated as the therapeutic considerations are different. Is the patient characterologically or impulsively psychopathic? Meaning, are they characterologically psychopathic at a baseline level of functionality, or are they, at times, impulsively psychopathic as a reaction? This distinction between trait psychopathy and impulse psychopathy will be explained in the next section.

Definition of characterological psychopathy

From my experience, a characterological psychopath is someone whose sole point of interaction with others is through their psychopathic traits – their existence and functioning in the world is entirely psychopathically structured. These individuals are innately disposed to snuffing out life – they cannot and will not appreciate growth and emergence, hence their menacing presence. They are organised around conceitedly watching life fail to the point of no return and smugly rejoicing in the knowledge that they are single-handedly responsible for this. This destruction needs to be a solo endeavour – to do it with another, or a group, would mean they would have to share the victory and its intensity. Neville Symington describes this action in isolation as an important diagnostic criterion for criminal psychopathy (1980, pp. 99–100).

According to Nancy McWilliams, a diagnosis of psychopathy "… refers to a basic failure of human attachment and a reliance on very primitive defences" (1994, p. 151); subsequently these defences reveal development that is arrested at the pre-verbal stage (McWilliams 1994, p. 98). This reliance on primitive defences is what distinguishes criminal psychopaths from other manifestations of psychopathy. Some people with primitive defences can operate in society and can, in fact, perform exceptionally well in corporate, legal and political arenas because they can also utilise more mature defences and have more identity integration and capacity to reality test in specific contexts (McWilliams 1994, p. 152). An example of this kind of socially adapted psychopath is 'Heathcliff', a central character in Emily Bronte's novel *Wuthering Heights*, discussed by Symington in his 1980 paper, 'The response aroused by the psychopath'. Heathcliff displays primitive defences, but he also has a capacity to contort his behaviour and appearance for social acceptance. This adaptation is not easily done by the criminal psychopath. They rely on primitive defences that result in their demise, and it is this manifestation of psychopathy that is my focus here, not the higher-order functioning psychopath.

I have found the following defences to be distinctive of criminal psychopaths in an institutional setting. This kind of psychopath must have 'omnipotent control' – they will always place themselves in a position where others are at their mercy, never the reverse. Given the opportunity, they will also unashamedly boast about how they have subjected others to states of total subordination and they assume that their listener will be impressed by their conquests. Despite appearing to be 'controlled' within an institutional setting, internally they have not lost control because they know, and are always dwelling on, what they are capable of – they know they can take a life at any time without remorse.

If they have killed or violated another, they perceive themselves and the other (or situation) through a dualistic, myopic lens of good and bad. This defensive 'splitting' occurs when there is an inability to consider and maintain ambiguity and uncertainty. Instead, they segregate the world into black and white, good and bad, right and wrong (McWilliams 1994, p. 99). The more developed version of splitting is 'moralising' (McWilliams 1994, p. 126) and the foundation for this defence is in binary thinking that then extends into moral judgements and justifications. According to Guggenbuhl-Craig, the psychopath's use of morality as a defence is necessitated by their lack of love – the less they can experience and embody love the greater the need to moralise. In this context, Guggenbuhl-Craig represents love as Eros, in reference to the Greek mythological God of Love. He states:

> [s]ince the compensated psychopath cannot depend upon Eros, his ego works out a moral system which is fool-proof in any and every situation. The result, as paradoxical as it may seem, is usually a well-developed morality with an emphasis upon the ego's role, but woefully lacking in love. Compensated psychopaths continually and at all costs uphold moral conventions, fanatically defending their moral systems. Were they to relax the hold on their moral code, the entire structure might well collapse like a house of cards, revealing their psychopathic nature.
>
> (1980, p. 108)

The final psychopathic defence I will discuss is 'projective identification' which can have a powerful impact on the therapist during and outside the sessions. The therapist can carry the psychopath's projections for years without fully comprehending the depth of what has occurred. This is explained by Symington when he says:

> [t]he psychopath projects his own inner despair into those around him and achieves his short-term goals in this way. He controls those around him through powerful projective mechanisms. He makes others feel what he dare not feel himself.
>
> (1980, p. 110)

Definition of psychopathic pocket

Characterological psychopathy is a distinctly disturbing cluster of traits, and the characterological psychopath is not shocked when they have an impulsive urge to destroy – it is familiar, perhaps experienced as the core of who they are. However, such an impulse is foreign to someone who is not structurally psychopathic but finds themselves at the mercy of an overwhelming desire to violate something or someone. This desire can unsuspectingly engulf a person to the point where they do not recognise themselves, and I refer to this other presentation as a 'psychopathic pocket'.

The term 'psychotic pocket' has been generally used to describe a 'mindless zone', suggesting being out of touch with reality. 'Pocket' is used metaphorically: it is attached to, or is part of, the clothes we wear, the bag or luggage we use, for the purpose of carrying something that is put in a protected isolated place that cannot be seen – it is kept in the dark. To extend the metaphor, psychopathic is specifically used as opposed to psychotic because when the person falls into such a pocket, their impulse is to violate and annihilate. Even though it is understood that a psychopathic pocket is also psychotic due to the disturbance or incapacity for reality testing, psychopathic is more accurate in instances when there is an intention to take destruction beyond the point of no return.

When a psychopathic pocket is triggered, it can manifest in a variety of ways ranging from behaviours of extreme aggression, violence and maniacal rage, to subtle alterations in the face or body. There can be an internal fantasy of destruction with no obvious indication of the murderousness that is being contemplated, or the mental wrestle to restrain the urge. When a person falls into a psychopathic pocket, they can be disturbed by the experience of complete otherness as it is at odds with how they have previously functioned in the world. They can be surprised at the extent to which they unwittingly embody psychopathy. Falling into a pocket can be experienced as either a fugue state, in which reality is suspended and they cannot fully grasp what they are thinking or control their behaviour, or they can have a conscious clarity and decide to go with their psychopathic tendency. Both manifestations can last for a significant period and have disastrous consequences if these impulses are acted upon.

The psychodynamic theories of Melanie Klein (1997) and Wilfred Bion (1962) provide valuable perspectives on aggressive and destructive forces, especially concerning the relational other and our desire to restore, repair, merge or control this other, in fantasy or reality. In contrast, my subject is the mind and inner workings of those whose specific and sole relational motivation is to obliterate the other, and then use their demonstrated capacity to obliterate and establish their sadistic authority as the basis of any other relationship. This history of obliteration is an omnipresent threat to whoever they associate with.

Unlike characterological psychopathy, which is rare, a psychopathic pocket can be experienced by a seemingly well-functioning person with no history of acts of violation or destructiveness. An individual can be forced beyond their emotional and intellectual competence to such an extent that a psychopathic pocket is activated. Giving birth, the early stages of parenting, death and dying, intimacy and sex, physiological alterations through using alcohol, substances and medications, and relationship issues are just some of the life experiences that can force someone, or someone witnessing another have this experience, beyond their functional threshold. Possible examples include 'crimes of passion', shaking of a screaming baby, a lethal maniacal rage towards oneself or another, or an altered internal state that fixates on torturing, tormenting or murder.

While dreadful crimes and catastrophic violations can be committed by both presentations of psychopathy, their outward functioning in the world can be vastly different. To illustrate this, I return to my case studies of Jimmy and Phillip.

Theoretical discussion of case examples

Case example 1 – Jimmy. Characterological psychopathy

It is interesting to note that even though my work with Jimmy occurred over two decades ago, the intellectual and emotional clarity in my countertransferential recall indicates the heightened nature of the encounter. Such is the permanent nature of the mark a psychopath can leave.

Jimmy was imprinted psychopathically; it was the only mode he operated from. Since conception, Jimmy's father viewed his unborn son as a 'little bastard' whom he did not ask for, let alone want, and he treated him accordingly. His father detested his mother's pregnancies, seeing them as her fault, and thus Jimmy, his brother and sister were an extension of the blame and resentment he felt towards her. Jimmy's mother was numb and vacant from her excessive use of alcohol, and she disengaged from her partner's violence towards their children, seeing it as their fault for getting in his way. Jimmy was disgusted that his mother was relieved when his father's violence was directed towards him and not her, as it meant she escaped it for that night. His father saw his children as pathetic and useless, giving him nothing. Consequently, he gave them nothing in return except floggings which served to vent his psychopathy. Jimmy's father used the earnings from his spasmodic employment as a truck driver and criminal activities purely for himself.

Jimmy despised his father, seeing him as all bad; that is, a violent monster, in contrast to himself, who was all good; that is, a righteous crusader. He projected this deep internal split onto the world seeing all existence as categorically black or white, good or bad, right or wrong. In Jimmy's mind there was an abuser and a victim, and he would either justify the behaviour of the perpetrator or defend the victim, according to whatever position suited him. Behind this was his moral hierarchy, his trusted barometer, and he accordingly extended this lens onto the other prisoners. Regarding addicts, he placed injecting meth users at the bottom of his hierarchy and recreational cannabis users that smoked joints (not 'bongs') at the top. In terms of crimes, child sex offenders were at the bottom, followed by break-and-enters, and this list would stretch to the highest level where Jimmy's honourable and distinguished crime was situated; that is, murder to protect a child while exposing crooked cops.

In relation to cognition, Jimmy's thinking was pre-symbolic, bordering on hallucinatory, as he arrogantly justified his behaviour from an indignant moral high ground. He spoke with conviction about how he had saved numerous victims by giving evidence of police corruption. He also considered that, through his act of murder, he had saved an 'abandoned girl' from her hopeless, drug-addicted mother. Jimmy's capacity to split and morally justify his actions meant he was unable to see his own act of murder as a continuation of his father's violence. Jimmy did not have the ability to access symbolic thought and entertain a perspective which was different from his. He overidentified with the story about the woman he murdered and took this information literally.

Residing in a protection cell in maximum-security with a daily allowance of one hour to exercise in a tiny yard was the environment Jimmy inhabited. There were regular staff shortages and union strikes which meant he would spend days or weeks at a time in this confined space. Many would see this existence as a form of torture, but not so for Jimmy. When he was in the community, he would routinely function solo. So, even prior to his incarceration, he had virtually no contact with others. His sister refused to see him as she had entered rehab and become dogmatically religious, and considered him a negative influence on her children. He had intermittent contact with his brother when he was not in gaol for drug-addicted crimes. His father had re-partnered and Jimmy had not seen or heard from him in over ten years, nor did he want to. His mother was barely alive, and was mostly bed-ridden with chronic alcoholic-induced medical conditions.

Jimmy's associations with people were the same in the community as they were in prison. His interactions were always transactional – he dealt with people on the basis that they were either *enforcing* the law or being *enforced* by the law. My role as therapist was not to enforce the law but to support people who were being enforced by the law, and I fitted into Jimmy's world accordingly. In our initial sessions I experienced Jimmy as speaking honestly and openly and I thought he was integrating and coming to terms with the deprivation and violence of his early environment. I assumed that his being imprisoned for the foreseeable future was a result of his background. Naïvely, I had deluded myself – Jimmy used me and the sessions as a playground to exercise his psychopathy.

When the therapeutic relationship began, Jimmy made the convincing impression that he was socially adequate through his infectious charm and charismatic authority. This presentation was curated with calculated intent. He playfully and manipulatively spun narratives of remorse and stories of his atrocious childhood. These were purely invitations that would seductively disarm me. When he felt I was sufficiently enthralled, he would lead me into the dark recesses of his psychopathic cruelty by exposing details of his malice towards unsuspecting and innocent people. Jimmy would repeatedly revisit the murder he was convicted of, and each time he would share a more disturbing feature, such as how she fought for her last breath. To be eligible for therapy while in prison, Jimmy had stated that he required sessions to help him learn to live with his remorse and guilt. For him, the sessions were a psychopathic indulgence under the guise of therapy.

Jimmy deceptively ingratiated himself with me through compliments about my non-judgemental approach and supportive listening. During the sessions, Jimmy seemed to relish watching me writhe as I metaphorically gasped for oxygen, my only hope being to desperately maintain therapeutic composure, but this would inevitably result in a split. I would attempt to seek refuge from my discombobulated state and feel sorry for him, taking the position of rehabilitator. Alternatively, I became the punisher, insisting he deserved to spend years behind bars. Whichever position I took, Jimmy won. He sensed my professional integrity was important to me, so this is what he annihilated on a weekly basis thereby gratifying his psychopathic need to torment and destroy. Then came his final victory – he killed himself, leaving a suicide note to me. Again, I was at his mercy.

Case example 2 – Phillip. Psychopathic pocket

As described earlier, Phillip's psychopathic pocket was not obvious until his third marriage. His pocket was 'camouflaged' by his army uniform and his destructive leanings were culturally condoned because they were in keeping with his military duties. An unconscious function of his employment was that it provided a structure and outlet for his tendencies. He spent years syphoning his aggression within the format of education and training in preparation for war. Having strict rules and regulations around violation provided the perfect arena for the psychopathic pocket to express itself through displacement. Phillip had a sense of the darkness he carried, but was convinced that all his colleagues experienced this because of the assimilated drills and what they had been exposed to. Furthermore, the military psychologist never raised any concerns about him when he participated in annual mandated counselling sessions. The context of his employment had led him to firmly believe that his internal annihilator was imperative for the preservation of himself and his colleagues.

When Phillip retired from the army, his compulsive searching on the internet for graphic, extremely violent war material was justified as an extension of many years of military training and involvement. Nonetheless, Phillip knew his obsessive viewing made him physically and psychologically lethargic and uninteresting, particularly because it was not something he could share with his wife or at social events. As retirement progressed his self-assurance deteriorated. He did not have his military status and subordinates to reflect his sense of importance, nor did he have mandatory fitness tests to secure his athleticism. It was only a matter of time before Phillip's façade would start to crack and the depression would worsen. The fear of this motivated Phillip to initiate and maintain more involvement with his grandchildren. He also knew that this behaviour would promote goodwill from his wife and children. The relationships with his children and grandchildren were not meaningful or satisfying for Phillip – he was aware that he did not delight in any of his offspring as the mother of his children did, nor as his current wife did towards her family. He was also aware that being honest about his ambivalence did not put him in a positive light, so he reluctantly maintained contact to preserve the pretence.

Phillip's first-born son Timothy was in his mid-30s with three children, the youngest being four months old. Timothy was the child with whom Phillip most strongly identified. They had numerous similarities including Timothy's insistence on being the sole financial provider so his wife could be home with the children. They also had parallel careers in law enforcement – Timothy joined the police force when he left school and had unwavering loyalty as a police officer. Their common language was morality, and the more they talked about hierarchical and institutional matters, the more Phillip was drawn to Timothy. Phillip had a sense of importance when Timothy asked him for advice on work-related matters and, on the odd occasion, his son would share his life stressors which required Phillip to share his experience of how he coped. However, Phillip was perplexed when Timothy and his wife asked him to be the guardian of their youngest son and he wanted to decline as he felt a sense of responsibility that overwhelmed him. In hindsight, it was the closeness that made him recoil. Phillip even used his ex-wife's potential disappointment as an excuse to decline the offer, to which Timothy replied, "that is her problem, we really want it to be you". Recognising that there was no way out, Phillip agreed.

The church chosen for the christening was over a century old and traditional in its practice. When Phillip entered the building he felt calm and was pleased to be there with his wife. He was proud to be ceremonially granted guardian and his wife was certainly impressed by this role. Towards the end of the service, he was ushered to join his son and daughter-in-law by the ornate sandstone font. The ceremony commenced, and the minister took his grandson and dipped the crown of his head gently into the water. As he did so, Phillip was engulfed by an urge to push the baby under the water and watch the bubbles from his mouth lessen until his flailing limbs flopped. As Phillip imagined doing this, he wanted to not only watch the baby's last breath, but also the look at the horror on the faces of his family. This was Phillip's psychopathic pocket, in his words, his darkness. He needed to turn the light of life into deathly dark:

> the moment of purity must be impulsively destroyed with the violent fantasy of annihilation because the unencumbered essence of another's authentic experience is intolerable and must be killed off and rendered lifeless.

Phillip's experience of his psychopathic pocket at the christening was completely unpredicted – it was an unconscious engulfment. Phillip felt like an internal imposter had possessed him and taken over his mind. He had unknowingly stepped on a psychopathic landmine and felt blown apart. Phillip's darkness had previously erupted when on a bush walk with his wife, as described earlier, and also at an alumni military function where he was sitting with his wife, nostalgically listening to the army band playing the songs that were the soundtrack of his army years. His contentment was palpable, and he invited his wife to dance. As a natural expression of their togetherness, Phillip's wife looked at him adoringly, just as she had when he experienced his first psychopathic pocket in reaction to her. As she did so, the music muffled in his mind, and he frantically scanned the room for a weapon. His stare locked onto a glass water jug that he could smash and plunge into her body, watching as she was terrifyingly at the mercy of the man she thought she knew and loved.

Although he fell into a psychopathic pocket in all three instances, there was a noteworthy difference in terms of his reaction following these incidents. In the examples on the bush walk and at the christening, he was horrified by his reaction and experienced it as an otherness within him. In the last example, he was disorientated and surprised by his reaction, but not horrified. Instead, he repeatedly recounted his psychopathic reaction in his mind, replaying what occurred with conscious intent and further imagining his wife's terror in detail. In his sessions, he presented this revisiting and replaying as problematic because the person he became in his repeated fantasy was at odds with his overall usual way of functioning. It was possible that his account of this dissonance was true, but my countertransference reaction alerted me otherwise. A subsequent example which confirmed my unease that Phillip's account was fraudulent was his rationalising that his voyeuristic internet trawling was to keep up-to-date with global military activity. This was clearly a justification that he talked himself into believing.

After eight months of therapy, Phillip seemed confident that I was not seriously disturbed by his psychopathic pockets or condemnatory of how he had conducted himself throughout his life, and on this basis, he assumed correctly that I was committed to our work. This relieved his fear of me leaving him. What did disturb me was how, when Phillip recounted his cruelty, he became chillingly void of affect. He would ever so slightly tilt his head up and look down as he smugly observed me. In this sequence I metaphorically became the maimed soldier at his mercy, his laser stare paralysing my clinical and theoretical mind. However, over time, my body and mind regained clarity and I was able to develop a hypothesis about the dissonance of his functioning and make sense of my countertransference responses.

My hypothesis was that Philip had to merge with authority (mother) and, at times, merge with the violent perpetrator (father) to ensure his psychological and physical safety. He had unconsciously protected himself throughout his military service by enforcing and upholding the rules, and when instructed, executed sanctioned violence. As a result of merging with his internalised parents, he could keep his grief at a distance, particularly his mother's abandonment of him. I was able to think about our work and hold onto my private mind with which Phillip could not merge in his attempt to protect himself from rejection and loss. This experience of another having a separate mind that he could not merge with was unsettling and intimidating. This was a reversal of positions and now Phillip was unnerved by me.

At a subliminal level, Phillip knew he was losing his psychological footing. He wanted to be genuine, retire with integrity, and be honoured as an esteemed ex-army officer. On the surface, he looked as though he had achieved this distinguished position. However, he knew deep down that this was a façade and it had an expiry date. The darkness within him was a malignant disease that he was managing through compulsive viewing of war footage. The only way he could enter remission was to look at his psychopathic pocket honestly and open himself to becoming conscious of the darkness that impulsively took over and destroyed moments of beauty and vulnerability.

Murder and other extreme violations are not only performed by someone who is characterologically psychopathic; they can also be enacted by someone who is overcome by a psychopathic pocket and acts accordingly. This presentation can appear in private practice or in other community settings, as there is more likelihood they have a sense of relational responsibility, in contrast to a characterological psychopath who has none, and will only seek treatment for litigious reasons such as court requirements regarding criminal activity or parenting matters. The psychopathic impulse is the same for both presentations but there are other similarities beyond this description that are worth considering, as well as some fundamental differences.

What are the differences and similarities between characterological psychopathy and a psychopathic pocket?

The case examples of Jimmy and Phillip offer instances to illustrate how the similarities of these presentations can manifest as differences.

Cruelty to animals in childhood

Animals are vulnerable, dependent and defenceless. Most importantly, they will struggle to stay alive and, for this reason, they provide the perfect outlet for a child with developing psychopathic tendencies to experiment on. They can start to exercise power and control as they torment an animal to death. Jimmy and Phillip both displayed obvious cruelty towards animals. The difference was that Jimmy used the ducklings he bludgeoned as a means to relish his classmates' distress. He recalled this story in our sessions so he could cause me anguish which fed his psychopathy. He had to be the cruellest person in the room, so he would never be the one who was vulnerable and at the mercy of another. In contrast, when Phillip's brother threatened to tell his mother that he had strung up a dog to a tree, he immediately stopped, fearing the reaction of another. He had no intention of killing the dog; by imitating his father's cruelty, he was attempting to regain control and, at some level, he overidentified with the strung-up dog. When he repeated this story in the session, he was timid and cautious and if I had reacted judgementally or distressed, I imagine he would not have continued his recollection.

The use of narcissistic defences

In both presentations of psychopathy there is an accompaniment of powerful narcissistic defences, namely 'imaginary' thought, "… a misuse of imagination for the purpose of denying everything that opposes the subject's desire" (Colman 2006, p. 23). This defence is a form of anti-symbolic thought that blocks out reality (covered extensively in Chapter 2) and when this is combined with psychopathic intent, the door opens for omnipotent violation, either behaviourally or in fantasy.

Jimmy's 'imaginary' thoughts were literal and concrete and his view of the world was how the world was. He was told a woman was neglecting and abusing her daughter and, to his mind, this entirely justified him committing murder. Jimmy had no access to an alternative perspective that did not fit his frame of reference and he had no reliable capacity to reality test. In contrast, Phillip's psychopathic pocket, although fleeting, did overwhelm him, and there was access to a part of himself that could assert itself and engage in the internal wrestle that held onto the consequences of his actions. In both cases there was a blocking out of reality which could be considered as a defence of dissociation or a trait of dissociative personality disorder (McWilliams 1994). This leads to questions about whether Jimmy was in a dissociative state when he committed murder and whether Phillip's psychopathic pocket is dissociative.

Jimmy's responses and reactions were consistently psychopathic in a way that I describe as characterological because when he violated others, he was considered and calculated and not in any way dissociated. When he narrated these violations, he never said anything that indicated he could not remember what happened or could not account for his actions. This is why I describe Jimmy's psychopathy as narcissistically based rather than dissociative. In the case of Phillip, there is questionable evidence of some form of dissociation as he enters a fugue state when he is overwhelmed and experiences an otherness that overcomes him. However, I describe his psychopathic pocket as a narcissistic defence because there is no evidence of a dissociative sub-personality or personalities, or an alter-ego. Also, the other reasons are that when Phillip is triggered, he does not cut off emotionally; instead, his emotional state is more acute. His reaction is not generalised, it is a direct result of being adored, loved and admired by the intimates in his life, not by anyone or anything else. Finally, his reaction is consistently psychopathic in nature and he does not have varied reactive states, thus the term narcissistic defence is used, not disassociation.

Distortion of authority

Another similarity in both of these cases is their experiences of distorted authority. As McWilliams observes, "[w]eak, depressed, or masochistic mothers and explosive, inconsistent, or sadistic fathers have been linked with psychopathy, as have alcoholism and other substance abuse in the family of origin" (1994, p. 156). This quote depicts both sets of parents: neither Jimmy nor Phillip had an internal reference of a good, useable mother or father, thus their role models for adult power were disproportionate and cruel and healthy authority was distorted. However, the manifestation of their distorted authority was not alike.

Jimmy's father was sadistic and cold-blooded and so was Jimmy. He could not see that his murder of a defenceless woman was a continuation of the violence he experienced at the hands of his father. According to Jimmy, he was nothing like his father. He saw himself as extremely honourable with a strong sense of morality; he was a righteous crusader, he was all good and his father all bad. In contrast, Phillip's impression of authority was shaped by his cruel mother and weak father. His mother would threaten Phillip and then enlist her husband to execute the violence. This outsourcing of violence translated into Phillip as an adult. In his profession he strictly adhered to the rules of the army, fearing the repercussions from his superiors if he was to transgress them. The army regulations were an omnipresent (maternal) threat that controlled him through fear, and when he was instructed, he followed through with the (paternal) execution. Phillip's moral compass was externalised and given to whoever was in power – in his mind they held the rules and he followed them without questionable discernment – whereas Jimmy's moral compass was internalised and incontestable – the outside world had no bearing on his impulsive need to act out.

Throughout Part 1 the term psychopath has been used to highlight a person who is innately disturbed or has a pocket of disturbance. These cases are used to bring forth the point in the following part of whether severely pathological people can individuate, or if individuation will naturally occur through maturity that is inherent in life-span development.

Part 2 – Individuation and maturity, are they different, intersecting or the same? Can maturity lead to individuation?

The movement from childhood to adult maturity includes physiological and psychological progression and occurs naturally as part of life-span development. Mental health issues such as depression, anxiety and grief are experienced in this development as responses to life events. Mental health also refers to someone's inherent nature that may have tendencies towards other psychological states such as schizophrenia and bipolar disorder. Personality disorders, for instance narcissism and psychopathy, are also in the mental health category. A person's inherent structure will impact their capacity to integrate and manage losses and transitions that occur in their life. The topic of maturity needs to be explored to differentiate whether this process is separate from individuation. With this in place, there can be a discussion of whether a psychopath can individuate.

Maturity

As part of the aging process, people naturally experience a diminishment in hormone and energy levels which can significantly slow down the psychopath's tendency to act, as they simply do not have as much impulsive drive and physical strength to exert their power (McWilliams 1994, p. 154). These physical changes can lead to a reduction in behavioural and sexual violations and give the appearance that improvements have been made (Guggenbuhl-Craig 1980, p. 89). However, these outward changes do not reflect psychological maturity because the changes which have occurred are physical, not psychological. The process of slowing down can place a person in a better position for psychological maturity but there is certainly no guarantee.

Psychological maturity can occur with the passage of time through exposure to life's losses by experiencing their own and other's illnesses, vulnerabilities and dependencies. The process of growing old can force people to face their fallibility and come to the realisation that sickness and death cannot be negotiated. These issues are sobering and can contribute to a person's mental health coming into question. The process of psychological maturity can be extremely problematic for certain presentations of psychopathy.

Therapists often work with issues that are related to the struggles of maturation. However, the question needs to be asked whether the patient is grappling with maturation or individuation, and is there an intersection. These issues may present as the same, but the internal workings that drive this expression are different. In therapy, the patient's drive can be deceiving as explained by Giorgio Tricarico:

> There are patients, however, in which this function serves mostly adaptation. In such situations, the need to seek to control life's vicissitudes seems to be much stronger than the need to evolve and to look for meaning. … [i]n summary, when a person's basic needs revolve around security and an illusion of control over existence, the compensatory function of the psyche might serve mostly adaptation and result in a strong need to *not* individuate.
>
> (2016, pp. 464–465, italics original)

Considering this, maturity can be an adaptation to the hardships of life, and the patient can use therapy to reinforce their defences. Having an awareness of one's defences *is* a necessary part of treatment as they are integral in understanding one's family of origin and are essential when coping with life's stressors and transitions (McWilliams 1994, p. 97). However, if defences are used as a deceptive control over life's sufferings, then a pseudo-maturity is cultivated. This is 'defensive', and has an unconscious intent that serves as an "… avoidance or management of some powerful, threatening feeling, usually anxiety but sometimes overwhelming grief and other disorganising emotional experiences; and … the maintenance of self-esteem" (McWilliams 1994, p. 97).

The experience of losing control, emotional overwhelm and instability of self-esteem are synonymous with the process of individuation. The devastation of this unravelling may be an opportunity for individuation. In the next section the case examples of Jimmy and Phillip are used to explore some of the clinically relevant aspects of maturation and individuation.

Theoretical discussion of case examples

Case example 1 – Jimmy. Maturity and individuation

Due to the age Jimmy was when he died and his imprisonment, there was insufficient data to reflect on his physiological maturation. His confinement meant his physical fitness could not be assessed and the lack of access to women left his sexual prowess untested. In fact, neither of these areas were of any concern to Jimmy as he did not care about his physical appeal in ways that are typically associated with wanting to be attractive to women. According to Jimmy, he was a 'bad boy', and this provided an endless supply of women that he could have transactional sex with when he was in the community.

The expression of Jimmy's relational desires for anyone was purely for reasons of self-gratification; his relational loops for genuine interpersonal connection were cauterised. This was an impediment that thwarted Jimmy's development of psychological maturity as the opportunity for growth through life's developmental transitions was blocked. These points lead to the conclusion that there must be a level of psychological maturity for individuation to occur. Indeed, as Jung explains, a capacity for interpersonal relating is fundamental to individuation: "… the process of individuation must lead to more intense and broader collective relationships and not to isolation" (1971, para. 758). From a position of moral righteousness Jimmy positioned himself outside the collective. He was not morally accountable or answerable to anyone as he made his own rules and would change them to suit himself at any time. He was the dispenser of justice and was separate to and above mainstream morality.

As such, he had no impetus to be part of society and there was no incentive for him to engage in any psychological discovery that would support him to function within the social order. The process of self-discovery can be painstaking and is described by Jung:

> Self knowledge is an adventure that carries us unexpectedly far and deep. Even a moderately comprehensive knowledge of the shadow can cause a good deal of confusion and mental darkness, since it gives rise to personality problems which one had never remotely imagined before.
>
> (1970, para. 741)

Subsequently, if this exploration is to be in any way profound, the awareness of one's shadow must necessarily emerge. The topic of morality must also surface because we can only understand our own morals in relation to others. For Jung, the link between the shadow and morality is as follows: "[t]he shadow is a moral problem that challenges the whole ego-personality, for no one can become conscious of the shadow without considerable moral effort" (1969, para. 14).

Psychological exploration that includes the shadow can awaken a patient's individuation process as they grapple to reconcile or explain the ways in which their needs or desires are at odds with their morals. They struggle to resolve the truth that their actions will affect their loved ones, and this alone can plummet a person into individuation. However, this experience did not apply to Jimmy because he disowned his shadow entirely and projected it outwards, which served to reinforce his position on the periphery of the collective.

This stagnant state that Jimmy was in is described by Tricarico:

> In the case of a negative individuation process, the psychic development veers toward a destructive polarity. Zealous attachment to symbols concerning the myth of the hero, extreme ideologies, and religious beliefs often become the rigid container of a weak personality structure, characterized by what Otto Kernberg (1995) termed *malignant narcissism*. The contact with unconscious material, in these cases, might contribute to sadism, aggression, fantasies of extreme violence, paranoid thinking, perversions, and/or grandiosity. This kind of negative individuation is most likely to occur in patients who fall somewhere between narcissistic and antisocial personality disorders, in diagnostic terms.
>
> (2016, pp. 465–466)

Through this lens, Jimmy's extreme ideologies manifested as moral judgements and justifications that were righteously proclaimed with traits that were clearly personality disordered. When I listened to these declarations it was crucial that I suspended my desire to gratify Jimmy by seeing him as a tortured soul that needed rehabilitating *or* an evil monster that had to be punished. The intent of the therapy was to provide an opportunity for him to meet his conscience, even if only momentarily. For this to occur he would have needed to reflect and somewhat resist his urge to use the therapist as an outlet for his psychopathy. He needed to use the time and space that the sessions offered to sit with himself and what he had done, and to some degree touch on his moral responsibility. This is what a progression of maturity and potentially individuation would have entailed for Jimmy.

However, the motivating factor for Jimmy's therapeutic treatment was to relieve his boredom by indulging his psychopathic tendencies. Jung refers to the 'method', which I will discuss in the context of therapeutic treatment. He states:

> [i]n reality, everything depends on the man and little or nothing on the method. The method is merely the path, the direction taken by a man: the way he acts is the true expression of his nature. If it ceases to be this, the method is nothing more than an affectation, something artificially pieced on, rootless and sapless, serving only the illegitimate goal of self-deception. It becomes a means of fooling oneself and of evading what may perhaps be the implacable law of one's being.
>
> (1967, para. 4)

Within Jimmy's comment, "I like how you play strictly by the rules", was an astute reflection of who I was and how I conducted myself. He accurately identified that I held a deep respect for, and belief in, the boundaries of the analytic frame and therapeutic relationship. Jimmy knew I would not be open to bribes or be erotically seduced. My nature was reflected in this method. I also understood that when working with pathology as serious as Jimmy's, the method is paramount. The methodology of the analytic frame needs to be strictly adhered to as a self-preservatory anchor against the psychopath's cruelty and unpredictability towards the therapist's genuine character. Having a romantic view that a therapist's good nature will effect change and override the method is naive and dangerous to the therapist and the patient's treatment.

Jimmy knew I could do what he could not: I could be simultaneously caring and moral. I could work within the rules and hold a space for ambivalence, because I understood that the world and the people within it comprise various shades of grey. I was able to be therapeutically composed in the face of contradiction and inconsistency and not act punitively to relieve my tension of not knowing. My hypothesis was that my relational capacities as a therapist ignited his primitive envy, and in turn he had to destroy what was precious to me, because he could not find it in himself.

Potentially, the treatment for Jimmy was for him to entertain and consider a perspective that was different from his own, which would in turn place him in a position to individuate or at least develop some relational maturity. I certainly attempted to not gratify his demand of taking a position of rehabilitator or of virtuous authority. My refusal was an endeavour to take the theatre out of his aggrandising psychopathy, and give him the opportunity to be in the room with another and not use them for his own indulgence. I wanted Jimmy to know that I would maintain composure and bear witness to him touching his conscience and contemplate how he would live with what he had done, and whether he could live with the knowledge that he had left a daughter motherless. I wanted him to consider whether he could live with his destructiveness and its consequences.

Unfortunately, the damage of Jimmy's history gave him a narrative of justifying his actions for the greater good. He only saw himself as an avenging angel who had saved a young girl from her abusive mother. I can only speculate that my capacity for holding his traumatic history, subsequent psychopathy, and the invitation for moral responsibility was intimidating. There was the possibility that Jimmy's engagement with me was the closest experience of respect, kindness and accountability that he has had with another. If any part of this speculation is valid, then Jimmy would have been at risk of glimpsing an emotional layer of sorts between two people. Another basis for this speculation was Jimmy's declaration during sessions, "gotta go, time's up" and he would abruptly walk out. He would foreclose any opportunity for vulnerability or not being in control.

Jimmy wrote a suicide note to me that described me as a 'very good listener' and that there was 'nothing I could have done'. My work with Jimmy has profoundly affected me as a person and as a professional, and I will continue to reflect and deliberate on this relationship. True to Jimmy's psychopathic form, he penetrated me to my core in a way that I will not be able to forget or have restful resolve. As a therapist there is always the potential for a patient to suicide and therefore the space that is being provided for individuation is potentially deadly. To deliberate the exact reason or reasons why Jimmy killed himself would be a violation of his sacred inner world and I do not want to perpetuate his violence by 'killing him' through claiming to know why he suicided. I am also aware of the trap of feeling guilty that I 'killed him' because of his incapacity to feel guilt and remorse about his actions. As McWilliams describes:

> [t]heir inability and/or disinclination to express emotions verbally means that the only way they can get other people to understand what they are feeling is to evoke that feeling in them.
>
> (1994, p. 154)

Guilt and remorse are emotions that are intrinsic to moral discernment, and for this reason the process of individuation for Jimmy was foiled. In contrast, the following case example of Phillip will present how the un-comfortability of experiencing guilt and remorse can provoke individuation.

Case example 2 – Phillip. Maturity and individuation

Both Phillip and Jimmy spent years in institutions that were bound by strict moral codes, but their internal and external relationships to morality were at odds. Confinement affected their psychological and physiological maturity very differently. Despite being 30 years older than Jimmy, Phillip exceeded his confinement and lived in the community. He faced what Jimmy did not, including being forced (by his age) to retire from the institution that cushioned him from some of life's realities.

Phillip entered his early 60s, and this demanded a certain maturation that he could no longer avoid. Admittedly, he did look younger than his chronological age, as he was physically fit from years of rugby training and the army's fitness requirements. The instruction for military parades also required he maintain an upright posture for hours, and this gave him a vigorous poise. However, his spinal rigidity dwindled and when he was not socialising he would round his shoulders and slump, especially when he was in front of a screen. He reluctantly admitted he had become a portly middle-aged man who had lost his sexual prowess and associated swagger. The effects of Phillip's aging could not be mistaken, and this consequently led to his fears of being alone – the impetus for seeking therapeutic support.

As described earlier, he wanted the therapy to reinforce his defences and polish his veneer. To Phillip's dissatisfaction, events took a course which was different to what he had envisioned or wanted, with psychological maturity having an unexpected beginning. The recollection of facts, experiences and emotional content was only available from the time Phillip joined the military as, according to him, this was when his life began. His life was subdivided into 'pre-' and 'post-' armed forces and any details prior to the army, such as his childhood or adolescence, were simply irrelevant as they had no bearing on the man he had become. Phillip's role in the army sustained his belief that he was publicly revered, and he thought his military status provided an amulet for some of his lifestyle misdemeanours.

Retirement was confronting for Phillip as he had nothing to do. He reluctantly understood that his repeated viewing of internet footage was a pathetic attempt to merge with historical memories of power and status. It was simply an outlet for his projections and fantasies that turned brutality into heroism. Phillip was embarrassed by this obsessive behaviour as he could see the juvenile quality in it. He imagined what his wife and son would think of him if they discovered his well-hidden indulgence. This imagining from another's perspective triggered his emotions of fear and shame: Phillip was psychologically maturing. An obvious example was when he would see his wife wince with pain from her arthritic hip and become distressed by her suffering. What touched him was her capacity to not complain and 'soldier on' – he admired her stoicism as a shared trait. Phillip could not escape the vulnerability that comes with aging and he and his wife mirrored each other's physical deterioration in her arthritic hip and his sporting injuries. The steadfast commitment Phillip demonstrated to supporting his wife through her upcoming hip replacement reflected his maturing relational responsibility.

There was a strange satisfaction for Phillip when he started to put the psychological pieces of his puzzle together. This searching and understanding culminated in Phillip developing a relational language that created an exclusivity with his wife, which he never had with previous wives. This interior language also gave him confidence to express a perspective on children and parenting when he spoke with his son Timothy. Phillip feared his new dialect would repel his wife and son, but instead they softened towards him. His wife was confused and concerned about the length of time he was in therapy and was surprised by the severity of his issues, as he never previously alluded to the extent he had been impacted by his history. Nonetheless, his wife was not threatened by his engagement in therapy, such was her profound respect for the man she married. Phillip was also surprised with what therapy had unveiled, specifically that he had no prior understanding that joining the army served as a distraction and adaptation to his unprocessed history.

This description of Phillip's work exemplifies a progression of his physical and psychological maturation. It also makes the point that for someone to be susceptible to individuation they must have a certain openness towards maturity. There were clearly quantifiable benefits that resulted from Phillip's therapy, but no matter how committed and compliant he was, the darkness would not go away. He still experienced his psychopathic pocket and was at the mercy of the overwhelming urge that would occur most strongly around his grandchildren and wife. Phillip was flummoxed by his impulsive need to violate the people in his life that he had grown to appreciate and enjoy. The despondency he felt towards this cruel urge eroded his once-reliable ego and gave rise to a tsunami of regressed emotions. He felt as though he had been transported into a mausoleum of atrophied fragments. As he blindly stumbled through the dark recesses, he stepped closer and closer to an understanding that was both reassuring and disturbing. Phillip's work, most notably the association with individuation, lasted over six years, and the following is a distilled version of a painstaking and liberating psychological excavation that Phillip worked through.

When Phillip was talking about viewing war footage in one of our first sessions, he commented that "there is so much beauty in the warzone", and when I asked him what he meant, he did not know. In hindsight, the meaning of his comment was that he was searching for some beauty of *his* birth within the warzone. According to Phillip's mother, his birth destroyed her. His entry to the world stopped her from living the life she had dreamed of as a young girl. She longed to be an educated woman with a career and have a wealthy husband to experience everything that her poor struggling parents could not. This fantasy for her future came to an abrupt end when she was 18 years old and became pregnant to Phillip's father, who felt entirely responsible and demonstrated his regret with a swift proposal and subsequent marriage before their baby was born. Phillip's inception crushed his mother's future fantasies. She was forced to uphold generational Catholicism, be a mother and marry a man she did not choose. She deeply resented her pregnancy and hoped to miscarry.

There was no genuine celebration of Phillip's birth, and he was certainly not delighted in. As a compensation for not being wanted he unconsciously learnt how to provide a 'service' to justify his existence. One of the functions he fulfilled was to be his mother's emotional dumping ground for her unprocessed emotions. Not only would she unjustifiably punish Phillip, but she would also punish her husband by getting him to execute her requests of violence. She knew her husband loathed enforcing her demands as they were contradictory to his passive and caring nature. Phillip's father's violence was fraudulent and duplicitous because it had not naturally arisen from within him, but instead was a submission to his wife's orders that served to preserve his archaic guilt. For Phillip, being the recipient of his father's violence was confusing because there was no conflict or disagreement between them and there was no emotional atmosphere that indicated a potential outburst. Instead, it simply appeared without warning or escalation. Phillip's psychopathic pocket was a repeated version of this violence.

As the therapeutic work continued, the psychopathic pocket became a known entity and there was an understanding of its likely origins and the reasons why it needed to express itself in certain circumstances. Phillip understood his psychopathic pocket protected his melancholic wound and was a reaction against it. His wound encapsulated his embodied unrest of not being wanted and subsequently rejected, and the painful reality of his mother's hope that he would die in her womb.

In contrast to Phillip's familial environment, the therapeutic setting offered what his family did not. His arrival was welcomed, the relational space was not encumbered with blame, and he was not resented. The therapeutic relationship provided an experience of careful holding, and the cruel mother that served the orders was absent. Instead, he had ongoing contact with a responsible transferential mother who was interested in how he put his world together, which included the processing of his unmourned loss of his birth mother and his feelings of confusion and anger towards his father. The therapy gave him insights into his life, as well as an experience of a relationship that did not end in abandonment or rejection, but instead demonstrated commitment to providing Phillip with what he needed from a relationship. Phillip's marriage also gave him what his family had not; his wife was loving and accepting which made him extremely uncomfortable. Both relationships placed psychological pressure on Phillip as they confronted his early attachment of love and relating which brought significant grief. The following two vignettes provide theoretical perspectives to illustrate how the process of individuation occurred in Phillip's life.

Engaging with the process of individuation

Phillip's employment afforded him a very comfortable lifestyle. This was reflected in the location and house he lived in, the education his children received and the fine-dining social events that were routinely offered by his employer. In contrast, his wife had independent wealth. Her high standard of living was a direct result of independent earnings, not from taxpayers, and because of this Phillip felt inadequate. When he attended the social events organised by his wife's friends his impeccable social etiquette masked his self-perceived incompetence.

Following the speeches at one of these lavish parties, Phillip was caught off guard and commented to his wife, "I am less of a man than your friend's husbands, I'm not successful and rich like all your friends are. I can't give you what they give their wives". To this she replied,

> And none of them will ever be able to dance like you, they could never be the first one on the floor and have everyone watching them, and wishing they could dance like you. I am lucky to be with you.

Phillip's wife had spontaneously responded to his expression of inadequacy. He knew she was genuine, and that she saw a quality in him that set him apart from other men, and she loved him for it. In that moment he experienced some breathing space that allowed him to take in what she had said. Phillip still felt an impulse to spoil, but instead of acting on it, he simply noticed it.

Phillip attributed the reduced strength and frequency of being overwhelmed by his psychopathic pocket to the work he had done in therapy. He came to understand that his wife's spontaneous displays of unconditional appreciation towards him could activate his melancholic wound. When she was enlivened by him, he experienced pain which would make him want to lash out and, over time, he came to understand this impulse as the pain of the baby who could not bring his mother to life. In those moments, his wife became his mother, the tormentor, and he felt her expression of love as a sadistic attack and therefore he needed to annihilate her.

The therapeutic unravelling of Phillip's psychopathic pocket reduced its intensity and he was able to experience the *reverberation* of it, as opposed to being taken over by it. He could feel a part of himself that could orientate his awareness to reality while simultaneously experience the impulse of the psychopathic pocket. These two possibilities created internal conflict, one being familiar with a predictable outcome, and the other being unfamiliar and unknown. He was in a dichotomous position, as described by Tricarico:

> ... increasing the degrees of freedom can be absolutely scary to some individuals ... to evolve would result in a much more difficult situation ... giving up omnipotence, no longer feels in control of what life brings about. For some patients, the possibility of pleasure or a moment of happiness may be very difficult to tolerate, as pleasure and happiness are fragile, unstable, and difficult-to-control conditions.
>
> (2016, p. 465)

Phillip sensed that it was his wife's love that was intolerable. To receive her adoration and delight in him meant resisting the urge to destroy, and that would place him in a position of vulnerability. As Phillip lay in bed after the lavish party, he kept replaying in his mind the compliments his wife had paid him about his dancing, and how she spoke with such innocence. He felt upset for her that he had portrayed himself as something he was not. He was scared that if he did not take the risk to give and receive love, it would only be a matter of time before this false portrayal would be exposed. He also felt overwhelming grief at having manipulated his wife's unguarded love to protect himself.

Progression towards individuation

It was impossible for Phillip to sleep as he had no distractions from his thoughts and feelings. After hours of tossing and turning he summoned up his omnipotence and scrolled the internet in search of war footage. He desperately tried to maintain equilibrium through displacement, which "... refers to the redirection of a drive, emotion, preoccupation, or behaviour from its initial or natural object to another because its original direction is for some reason anxiety ridden" (McWilliams 1994, p. 130). Phillip's melancholic wound had been exposed and, to some extent, cathected, which meant there was minimal drive that needed to be redirected. The defence mechanism of displacement had been disabled. Watching war footage did not provide the relief that Phillip had intended, as evident in his account:

> I went to another level, I watched a soldier lying on the ground and pleading for his life, the perpetrator must have had a camera mounted on him, and this defenceless soldier was begging and begging to be saved. Then there was this moment, he surrendered, he gave up, he took a deep breath and as he turned away, he closed his eyes. Then he was shot dead. This is seriously messed up, I don't know what the world has come to, but I am a part of this, I am perpetuating this.

Phillip felt ashamed of himself as he could no longer deny that he used defenceless, pleading men for his own selfish gain. He clearly understood that the intent of his voyeurism was to merge with the power and status he once had, and to stimulate and encourage his psychopathic pocket. This footage, however, violated a human taboo. The soldier he scrutinised was completely vulnerable and exposed – he was in a state in which a person is in their most animalistic form, when they are on the threshold of death and their body takes over. It was an intimate moment for the solider, he needed his privacy and looked away to die. But his profound experience was invaded and polluted for personal gain by Phillip and countless other voyeurs. Phillip was aware he had broken the code of humanity and had given someone the ultimate disrespect.

After Phillip watched the footage, he noticed he experienced an entirely different response. This time he did not merge with the sadistic dominance of the perpetrator but instead connected with the powerless vulnerability of the soldier, whose life had been mercilessly taken away. The footage mirrored the kernel of Phillip's psychopathic pocket, a truth that he had spent years unearthing in therapy. Phillip understood that his exploitation of another's annihilation was inherently inhumane.

The unconditional care Phillip received from his wife and the respect from his son gave him hope of an alternative way of living – a life that was not motivated by his psychopathic pocket. As time passed, he did have an emerging sense of an alternative. Phillip described his situation: "I am aware of this entity that draws me in to be a better person, and I know it is about love. I realise I have exiled myself from love – it's me who would not let it in".

Individuation for Phillip meant resisting the psychopathic impulse to spoil the moment and kill it with cruel intent, to destroy the opportunity for intimacy or connection with himself and others. The alternative to spoiling was to tolerate the unknown of the moment, be present to the experience, and be curious about what will emerge. This letting go of control and openness to an 'entity' is described by Jung: "I was being compelled to go through this process of the unconscious. I had to let myself be carried along by the current, without a notion of where it would lead me" (1995, p. 222). The process and outcome of individuation is further explained by Claire Dunne as:

> … the experience of a natural law, an inner self-regulating process by which man becomes a whole human being acknowledging and living the total range of himself. In the process the ego is ultimately faced with something larger than itself, a force that it yields to and serves. The human being thus recognizes itself as both material and spiritual, conscious and unconscious.
>
> (2012, pp. 83–84)

When possessed by his ego Phillip assumed that what mattered was his psychopathic pocket which was 'larger' than himself and which he served by compulsively indulging in its destructiveness. However, this was not the 'something larger' that authentic individuation refers to. When Phillip's ego resisted the impulse arising from his psychopathic pocket, he came to know what was genuinely greater than himself which was a sense of love. Individuation for Phillip was to experience receiving and giving love: this is what he needed to yield to for his psychic development.

The recognition of material and spiritual, conscious and unconscious is what Phillip interpreted as the entity that drew him to be a better person. He understood the dichotomy that was repeatedly presented to him, that his ego sought familiar expression by spoiling and destroying. At the same time, the entity required him to resist that impulse and instead, let go of control and be present to the moment. Either he had to let the current carry him or forcibly swim upstream.

Even though he had become increasingly aware of his options, Phillip did not feel he had a choice. He knew that fostering his relationship with his psychopathic pocket would ultimately lead to destruction as he would annihilate himself with his own cowardice. His choiceless alternative was to courageously be open to love, and to harness a sense of the entity within. This alternative was certainly not a 'quick fix' that would end in cure. The lived reality of Phillip being open to giving and receiving love is explained by Guggenbuhl-Craig:

> Let there be no mistake: Eros is no savior; he is not the key to living "happily ever after". While Eros makes the archetypes more human, tempering their demonic qualities, he himself can be quite demonic. Much of life's tragedy and comedy, sadness and joy, despair and jubilation arise out of the conflicts and confusion which Eros evokes. To be in love, with someone or something, leads to suffering, conflict, problems, and frustrations … but to joy and satisfaction as well.
>
> (1980, p. 28)

Love, otherwise known as Eros, was what Phillip experienced when he allowed himself to be vulnerable and present to life. This openness led him to venture into unexplored areas of his psyche and feel the associated range of emotions. Consequently, his psychological and spiritual range became wider and more robust which was reflected in his expanding relational and moral responsibility. Phillip could now live from his own internalised moral and relational compass, as opposed to an externally imposed set of rules and expectations.

The choice to individuate or not was repeatedly presented to Phillip in everyday living, as overt or subtle invitations for humility or destruction. These were opportunities to live more fully into parts of himself or to close these areas off. Phillip's psychopathic pocket still caught him off guard, and its seductive enticement would at times be impossible to resist; however, there was a significant difference in terms of his relationship with this pocket. When he did meet this destructive force, he was not really interested in the content of it or replaying it for a sense of pseudo-power. Instead, he was curious about why it was triggered, the context and the reason it sought expression.

There is no happy ending with individuation as it "is never completed and remains an ideal concept" (Samuels 1985, p. 102). Phillip came to uphold self-responsibility – he pursued transparency and lived a life that was marked with spontaneity and complexity. His motivation to live in this way was largely from fear, as he knew the alternative was to stew in self-exiled loneliness and cowardice.

Can a psychopath individuate?

For this question to be answered the therapist needs to assess and consider the following factors:

Capacity for symbolic thought

Is the patient able to imagine how they have affected another person and their life, and what is the nature of these imaginings? A patient who sadistically replays the pain of their victim when they were at their mercy is completely different from a patient who can feel genuine guilt and remorse from imagining the pain they have inflicted on another.

Presentation of psychopathy

The therapist must evaluate whether they are working with someone whose functioning in the world is psychopathically structured, or whether the patient is periodically overcome by a psychopathic pocket. This distinction is imperative as the treatment outcomes and course of therapy are dependent on it.

Relationship to their offence

The relationship in question can be to their literal offence in which they violated someone or something, or to the imaginings of their psychopathic pocket: "It is not the deed which makes a person a psychopath, but his relationship to it" (Guggenbuhl-Craig 1980, p. 46). The patient's relationship to their offence can provide information about the presentation of psychopathy the therapist will be working with. The characterological psychopath will relive and indulge their offence, ultimately strengthening their bond to what they have done. Alternatively, the work may be focused on the patient understanding the multitude of factors that led to their act of violation. A crucial part of this process is remorse, and the question of how to live with what they have done. Individuation can be initiated by taking moral responsibility and subsequently atonement, or they can be included within the process.

Context

Due to the psychopathic inclination to breach societal and cultural boundaries, these people often come to the attention of health professionals and authorities in forensic, correctional and rehabilitation institutions. This detention makes them known to specialists and has the potential for them to engage in treatment. The 'brick mother' (Minne 2011) closes certain outlets and forces the patient into a quarantined environment where they must engage with certain services. The level of security and confinement may increase the need for treatment, and thus potential, for individuation. If they are not detained, society is a playground for those who are structurally psychopathic and offers minimal, if any, motivation to engage in any form of treatment.

What is motivating the question, can a psychopath individuate?

This question has an underlying nuance that infers an uncertainty about the effectiveness of treatment. The treatment must be scrutinised because a simple yes or no answer to this question indicates a lack of clinical interrogation and respect for the subject matter. The therapist must understand what their impetus is for asking this question, and ascertain the association between asking the question and the patient's stage of treatment. The therapist has a responsibility to continually evaluate their countertransference, projections and projective identifications, in particular the unconscious collusion with psychopathic and narcissistic defences. A clinical concern that can underlie the therapist's questioning of psychopathy and individuation is therapeutic heroism wherein they believe they can defy the odds and rehabilitate. They think they are the 'special therapist' but in fact, they have been seduced and have unconsciously become a pawn of the psychopath. The therapist's response to whether a psychopath can individuate can reflect who they are as a therapist, their experience with psychopathic patients, and the treatment they provide.

This question also brings to light the therapist's relationship with evil, and the reality that darkness is inside and outside us all, and that we must be able to 'be with' the helplessness and hopelessness of this aspect of the human condition. If a therapist cannot 'be with' and 'live with' this in both them and others, their asking of this question is likely to be ill-informed and risks being superficial.

When working with this type of patient in an institution, the therapist can be paralysed with primitive fear and their instinctual need for self-preservation can override the provision of effective treatment. Symington writes, "I do not offer a solution but it is healthier to recognise that very often we collude with the criminal psychopath for our own safety, and we should not deceive ourselves about it or blame others for doing so" (1980, p. 105). The therapist needs to be honest with themselves – they can be ashamed to admit they are comforted that their patient is in prison and never want them to be released.

The therapist must consider all these determining factors before they can directly address the question of whether a psychopath can individuate. Commenting on whether someone can or has individuated is fraught as it assumes the person who is asking the question is themselves individuated and can therefore assess someone else's individuation status. The process of individuation and living in an individuated way is private; ultimately, we each define what this process means for us as we grow into our personal and unique definition of it. Therefore, I can never say definitively whether someone can individuate or not as I am not an authority on another's deepest self and can never predict what may happen in a person's life that could radically change their psychological trajectory. What I can do is base my answer on clinical experience that will hopefully generate considerations and further questions.

A patient who is not structurally psychopathic but is overwhelmed by their psychopathic pocket has the potential to individuate, especially if they have an underlying fear that places them in a position of vulnerability. They must be in a predicament such that, if they do not change, they will be unable to live with the consequences. These fears can be and are often associated with maturity which is why developmental life stages and chronological age can force a surrendering of the ego, and an engagement with the individuation process may begin.

In contrast, for the characterological psychopath the ego is always in charge. They are inherently programmed to seek and violate someone's vulnerability and spoil their innocence. They insert their cruelty and take the life out of someone or something, and they evoke fear in others by preying on their vulnerability. They do not experience these emotions in themselves and the absence of emotions, specifically fear and vulnerability, renders them unmotivated to take the kind of relational and moral responsibilities which are fundamental to individuation. Thus, a characterological psychopath who is in the community has no likelihood of individuating. The only hope for psychological integration of characterological psychopathy is institutional confinement as this can reduce their outlets for indulging in psychopathic traits. Also, there is more probability of receiving treatment in a facility as opposed to when they are in society.

Consequently, my professional assessment regarding the question of psychopathy and individuation is that there is hope for a patient with a psychopathic pocket to individuate, but this hope is nominal (if it is there at all) for a characterological psychopath. However, this question is most effectively answered with reference to the treatment of the patient with whom the therapist is working, as this ensures that individuality is promoted and maintained.

Part 3 – Psychopathy and women

As I have already mentioned, my work in correctional institutions was with men. In this capacity I encountered only a handful of women in witness protection and some in the forensic unit who were considered psychopaths. Due to system-based factors (availability and time constraints), I did not get to work with these women at sufficient depth to think about their presentation as psychopathic. As such, the following is a discussion from my work in private practice with patients whose lives have been impacted by what I strongly speculate are female psychopaths. This sub-set of educated female patients sought treatment because of their encounters with this type of female pathology. While, for the sake of simplicity, the female perpetrator will be referred to as a psychopath, please keep in mind that these women were *allegedly* psychopathic – they were not my primary patients and consequently my diagnosis is hypothetical.

Reflections – Psychopathy and women

I am categorising these women in this way for the same reasons that I previously identified in psychopathic men: their traits and actions lack emotion. They callously destroy as an end in itself and revel in the knowledge that they have gotten away with whatever cruelty they have inflicted. These women are characterologically psychopathic as their actions are conscious and deliberate, they have a complete failure of empathy, they are sadistically stimulated as they smugly observe how they have disabled their victim, and they delight in the damage or loss of life function they knowingly caused.

The concept of the psychopathic pocket does not apply to these women as their actions are conscious and calculated. On the rare occasion they are caught, they claim amnesia or mental health problems as an excuse, and will protest their innocence with conviction. The women I am referring to as psychopaths may not meet the diagnostic criteria because of their social adaptation, but their actions certainly correlate with those of the characterological psychopath. In these cases, it is *only* the psychopath and their victim that know the true nature of the violation. If the victim shares their experience, they are rarely believed, or only partially believed as the truth seems so bizarre as to be incomprehensible.

A noteworthy difference between male psychopaths and educated, or at least somewhat educated, female psychopaths is that men want to physically kill or, if they themselves cannot kill, they want their victim dead, completely dispensed of. In contrast, women psychopaths want to (as it were) inject deadly or severely debilitating poison into their 'prey'. If they cannot get to their victim directly, they will try to harm or damage their victim's loved ones. This usually does not end in literal death, but it can. Regardless of the form of the attack, the outcome is always irreparable suffering, and the psychopath triumphantly relishes in the damage she has done.

The female psychopath is driven by 'primitive envy': they desire what someone else has and, because they do not have it, they need to spoil or destroy it (Klein 1997). At some level they know someone – usually a family member or very close friend or associate – has something that they lack. This deficit is not known to the psychopath or victim at the beginning of their mutually beneficial relationship and a form of enmeshment masks the psychopath's lack. It is only when the victim dares to psychologically develop and begin to separate from the relationship that the psychopath's lack becomes evident. It is the victim's separation that ignites the psychopath's primitive envy, and they retaliate by exerting increasing and, if possible, omnipotent control. The victim is often confused by the psychopath's reaction and can start to question and doubt themselves. Once it is evident to the psychopath that the victim will not be returning to their web, they will commence calculated attacks to: firstly, attain and destroy what the other has; secondly, punish them for having what they do not; and thirdly, punish them for leaving.

It can be near impossible for outsiders to understand and believe how the psychopath can insidiously corrode another person. The presentation of this style of psychopath is one of social acceptance; they are often financially generous and provide unwavering emotional support for the small group of female friends that surround them. Unlike the criminal male psychopath who operates in isolation, this style of female psychopath collects a posse of dependent and needy friends who idealise and rely on their guru and blindly support her. They are devoted followers, striving to attract sentimental compliments from their revered leader. These friends are oblivious that they are used as amulets by the psychopath, as is their partner who is usually passive and weak.

The victim may have been part of the posse or in an exclusive relationship with the psychopath. Regardless, when they distance themself from the clique, they will be discredited as the psychopath banishes them and persuades others to disown them also. When the victim sees they are ousted and are aware that this is because the psychopath is threatened by their growth and independence, they become frightened and know they must move away for their own safety and sanity. The psychopathic traits emerge and become more obvious to the victim who can distance themself emotionally and intellectually, and will continue to do so as they become more psychologically sound, but if the psychopath is a family member or part of their social or professional sphere, they may be unable to completely detach from them. If the victim does manage to step away it is usually to no avail; the psychopath's deviousness *will* reach them and have permanent consequences.

If the psychopath cannot have direct access to their victim because their victim has moved away for self-preservation, they will operate through triangulation, and the third is punished. In most cases the third is a baby, toddler or adult child of the victim, and the psychopath uses the offspring of the victim as their weapon. They create 'parental distress'. They know that if they tamper with the child's innocence, they will undoubtedly get the attention of the one who has left them to regain their power and control. The 'baby' can be literal or metaphorical – an animal, business, career or activity – it is always something, someone or a group that is extremely important to the victim and they are committed to protecting its vulnerability and nurturing its development. Even though it may not be a literal baby or child, when it is threatened, parental distress is deeply felt.

It is an ugly, almost unthinkable reality that women can treat other women with such cruelty and abuse their children. This abuse can take a range of forms including psychological and/or sexual – whatever the medium, it is a transgression or violation of the child and creates parental anguish. Unlike the male psychopath who commits a crime because of his sexually motivated deviancy, sexual abuse, when perpetrated by a female psychopath, is not typically erotically motivated. The sexual element in female psychopathy is intended to destroy the innocence of the defenceless child and exploit them. The child is merely a pawn to the female psychopath whose aim is to repossess the envied person who has what they lack. Society turns a blind eye on women as sexual abusers, preferring to believe that women only behave like this under pressure from an abusive man. In some cases it can be quite the opposite, with the partner of the psychopathic woman being inadequate and oblivious, or colluding with her.

These psychopathic women often have roles in caring industries such as medical or mental health support, employed as nurses, psychologists, counsellors, childcare or social workers or teachers. They can volunteer in schools, or charities for the underprivileged, or can be involved in philanthropy. Their involvement in roles that are perceived to be caring and giving can add another layer of unbelievability to what they are capable of, and this can be used as another amulet to disguise their underlying nature.

Similarly situated in the caring professions, therapists work on the fragile edge of their personal and professional boundaries, not only with themselves but also with their colleagues and patients. The role of the therapist brings with it significant responsibility.

What is the responsibility of the therapist when working with presentations of psychopathy?

Working with psychopathy has consequences for the therapist, which are not always apparent until a serious, sometimes deadly, violation occurs. These consequences are not entirely preventable, but the extent of the harm may be reduced if the therapist is aware of this part of themselves and the risk of unconscious collusion with the patient. This includes the vicarious use of the patient and acknowledging the reality and severity of the psychopathic impulse that is part of the human condition.

The word psychopath typically elicits a response of panic and fear and has associated images and fantasies that change as one matures. The childhood version of these can be in the form of monsters, boogiemen or baddies who lay in wait under the bed or in dark places. Children play 'hide and seek' and 'cops and robbers' to integrate their emerging awareness of these dark characters within themselves. In adolescence, the association with psychopathy can present as an attraction to, or becoming, the bad boy, erotic dancer, drug addict or gangster. Another point of access to these dynamics is through movies, television, news, fictional and non-fictional literature. Whether these engagements are in actual life or internal fantasies, they are important and necessary for us to understand, and to integrate into our ongoing relationship to our darkness, psychopathy or whatever name we choose to give this part of ourselves.

When a therapist is working with psychopathic presentations they must take responsibility for this aspect of their own shadow. This is an uncomfortable process because, as Samuels observes:

> ... the integration of the shadow, implying acceptance of rejected, repressed and as yet unlived aspects of oneself is painful, particularly when what is involved is the withdrawal of projections on to other people.
>
> (1985, p. 102)

Consequently, the therapist must explore what they are projecting from their shadow and attempt to understand how psychopathy, or a psychopathic pocket, may manifest in their life – in reality or in fantasy.

If a therapist does not work with this part of themselves, they are vicariously using their patient to experience what it is like to live closer to the edge without having to face the consequences. They are syphoning onto their patients a vital part of what it is to be human, keeping life at a safe distance under the delusion that they understand psychopathy.

Through projective identification, the therapist can unconsciously embody the psychopath's emotions and associated states in their own life. The therapist can feel isolated and disenfranchised from their family and friends and become confused and depressed as to why they feel 'out of step' with their peers and society. Alternatively, the therapist may overidentify with the psychopath's 'specialness'. They may enact this as a false sense of importance and provide 'dinner party conversations' where they grandiosely share stories of patients. This grandstanding may be a way of violating the patient because the therapist has felt the same violation in the sessions, or they are using the patient because they feel uninteresting and can gain attention by using another's darkness instead of taking responsibility for their own.

An example of disowned processes for the therapist who works in an institution is when they leave their workplace and indulge in the knowledge that they have the freedom to go home every night to their comforts. Another manifestation is when the therapist is prejudiced – they may be unjustly punitive in their views on punishment or be a naïve and idealistic advocate for patients' or prisoners' rights. In either position, they are servicing their own unprocessed material at the expense of the people they are working with.

It can be psychologically and psychosomatically arduous for the therapist to hold the projections and projective identifications from their workplace and attempt to balance this with their everyday life. This is particularly apparent when there is the complication of death and suicide. Symington writes that "[t]he end justifies any means but there always is an end" (1980, p. 105). The tendency for the characterological psychopath to 'end' their life by suicide can be explained by them as always having to be in control. They are the master of their own life and death and are not bound by relationships or moral rules of existence. Their ultimate annihilation is a self-imposed murder whereby they put an end to their own life, as they cannot let life take its natural course and experience the vulnerability of being at life's mercy. In the cases of psychopathic suicide, the therapist may be left burdened by their involvement with the 'dark joker' and be forced into an inescapable labyrinth that leaves them no option but to confront themselves, personally and professionally.

Impending death can be different for other presentations of psychopathy. They may desperately and truthfully declare their wrongdoings, crimes or violations when they know they are going to die, because no matter what the denomination, there is a universal fear of 'going to hell'. As the patient is exposed and defenceless, they may be very open and sensitive and appear to be in the early stages of individuation. However, they are mostly reluctant to take responsibility and process their material – they are simply using the therapist as a confessional and someone to rid them of their baggage.

Given the variety of psychopathic presentations a therapist can work with, it is essential for them to take responsibility to understand how their work is manifesting and being expressed in their own life. They must be aware of their own shadow and avoid the potential scenarios discussed here.

Conclusion

This chapter has offered selected clinical and theoretical perspectives on psychopathy with the intention of encouraging the therapist to consider the dynamics and influences that underlie the question of whether a psychopath can individuate. Emphasis has been placed on the therapist not taking a defensive, binary position that adamantly proposes that change is impossible, or idealistically believes that change is always possible. It is the responsibility of the individual therapist to have an ongoing and discerning questioning of both these perspectives.

As discussed, a determining factor of the therapist's effectiveness is their ever-evolving awareness of, and accountability for, their own shadow and, more unsettlingly, their psychopathic pocket. This individual work is vital, as Jung explains, because:

> …we cannot be whole without this negative side, that we have a body which, like all bodies, casts a shadow, and that if we deny this body we cease to be three-dimensional and become flat and without substance.
>
> (1966, para. 35)

Consequently, a multi-dimensional therapist is one who takes responsibility for their unique edge and uses it as the basis of their clinical work. Integral to this is humility, and a capacity to bear not knowing in the service of the therapeutic encounter.

References

Bion, W. R. (1962). *Learning from experience*. London: Heinemann.
Colman, W. (2006). 'Imagination and the imaginary', *Journal of Analytical Psychology*, 51(1), pp. 21–41.
Dunne, C. (2012). *Carl Jung: Wounded healer of the soul*. London: Watkins Publishing.
Guggenbuhl-Craig, A. (1980). *Eros on crutches: Reflections on amorality and psychopathy*. Irving, TX: Spring Publications.
Jung, C. G. (1966). *The collected works of C. G. Jung. Volume 7: Two essays in analytical psychology*. 2nd edn. Edited by Read, H., Fordham, M., & Adler, G. Translated by Hull, R. F. C. Princeton, NJ: Princeton University Press.
Jung, C. G. (1967). *The collected works of C. G. Jung. Volume 13: Alchemical studies*. Edited by Read, H., Fordham, M., & Adler, G. Translated by Hull, R. F. C. London: Routledge & Kegan Paul, Ltd.

Jung, C. G. (1969). *The collected works of C. G. Jung. Volume 9 (part 2): Two essays in analytical psychology: Aion: Researches into the phenomenology of the self.* 2nd edn. Edited by Read, H., Fordham, M., & Adler, G. Translated by Hull, R. F. C. Princeton, NJ: Princeton University Press.

Jung, C. G. (1970). *The collected works of C. G. Jung. Volume 14: Mysterium coniunctionis.* 2nd edn. Edited by Read, H., Fordham, M., & Adler, G. Translated by Hull, R. F. C. Princeton, NJ: Princeton University Press.

Jung, C. G. (1971). *The collected works of C. G. Jung. Volume 6: Psychological types.* 2nd edn. Edited by Read, H., Fordham, M., & Adler, G. Translated by Hull, R. F. C. Princeton, NJ: Princeton University Press.

Jung, C. G. (1995). *Memories, dreams, reflections.* Edited by Jaffe, A. Translated by Winston, R., & Winston, C. London: Fontana Press.

Klein, M. (1997). *Envy and gratitude and other works 1946–1963.* London: Vintage.

McWilliams, N. (1994). *Psychoanalytic diagnosis: Understanding personality structure in the clinical process.* New York: The Guilford Press.

Minne, C. (2011). 'The secluded minds of violent patients', *Psychoanalytic Psychotherapy,* 25(1), pp. 38–51. United Kingdom: Taylor & Francis.

Samuels, A. (1985). *Jung and the post-Jungians.* London: Routledge.

Symington, N. (1980). 'The response aroused by the psychopath', *International Review of Psychoanalysis,* 7, pp. 291–298.

Tricarico, G. (2016). 'The individuation process in post-modernity', *Psychological Perspectives,* 59(4), pp. 461–472.

Conclusion

This book presents individuation as a powerful concept that can be applied to contemporary clinical work with a wide range of patients who present for therapy with a spectrum of conditions. It offers clinicians a perspective from which they can reflect on Jung's concept of individuation in a way that enables them to hold an overall picture of their patient, as well as the detailed operation of their defences against change and growth. My focus is on how we can help people whose opportunities for individuation are embedded in maladaptive ways of living and being.

DOI: 10.4324/9781003558125-7

Index

For Product Safety Concerns and Information please contact our EU
representative GPSR@taylorandfrancis.com
Taylor & Francis Verlag GmbH, Kaufingerstraße 24, 80331 München, Germany

www.ingramcontent.com/pod-product-compliance
Lightning Source LLC
Chambersburg PA
CBHW070350270326
41926CB00017B/4076

9 781032 904498